Cambridge Elements

Elements in Gender and Politics
edited by
Tiffany D. Barnes
University of Texas at Austin
Diana Z. O'Brien
Washington University in St. Louis

CONFLICT AND MATERNAL HEALTH

Linking the Gendered Causes and Gendered Consequences of War

Susan Hannah Allen
University of Mississippi

Frank C. Thames
Texas Tech University

Shaftesbury Road, Cambridge CB2 8EA, United Kingdom

One Liberty Plaza, 20th Floor, New York, NY 10006, USA

477 Williamstown Road, Port Melbourne, VIC 3207, Australia

314–321, 3rd Floor, Plot 3, Splendor Forum, Jasola District Centre, New Delhi – 110025, India

103 Penang Road, #05–06/07, Visioncrest Commercial, Singapore 238467

Cambridge University Press is part of Cambridge University Press & Assessment, a department of the University of Cambridge.

We share the University's mission to contribute to society through the pursuit of education, learning and research at the highest international levels of excellence.

www.cambridge.org
Information on this title: www.cambridge.org/9781009539586

DOI: 10.1017/9781009430616

© Susan Hannah Allen and Frank C. Thames 2025

This publication is in copyright. Subject to statutory exception and to the provisions of relevant collective licensing agreements, no reproduction of any part may take place without the written permission of Cambridge University Press & Assessment.

When citing this work, please include a reference to the DOI 10.1017/9781009430616

First published 2025

A catalogue record for this publication is available from the British Library

ISBN 978-1-009-53958-6 Hardback
ISBN 978-1-009-43065-4 Paperback
ISSN 2753-8117 (online)
ISSN 2753-8109 (print)

Cambridge University Press & Assessment has no responsibility for the persistence or accuracy of URLs for external or third-party internet websites referred to in this publication and does not guarantee that any content on such websites is, or will remain, accurate or appropriate.

For EU product safety concerns, contact us at Calle de José Abascal, 56, 1°, 28003 Madrid, Spain, or email eugpsr@cambridge.org

Conflict and Maternal Health

Linking the Gendered Causes and Gendered Consequences of War

Elements in Gender and Politics

DOI: 10.1017/9781009430616
First published online: November 2025

Susan Hannah Allen
University of Mississippi

Frank C. Thames
Texas Tech University

Author for correspondence: Susan Hannah Allen, shallen@olemiss.edu

Abstract: What impact does war have on women's well-being? War is far more likely to occur in countries where women lack equal standing in society. When those wars occur, the effects are also gendered. If gender inequality is affected by both the causes and impacts of armed conflict, we need to think about the implications of this interrelationship. Focusing on gendered political inequality, this Element takes a large-N approach to exploring whether inequality variation in states at conflict leads to variation in women's health outcomes. By linking the two processes, the authors are able to directly account for the impact of political inequality on which countries participate in civil conflict when they estimate the impact of inequality on conflict consequences, particularly those relating to women's health.

Keywords: gender, armed conflict, women's health, consequences of war, gender inequality

© Susan Hannah Allen and Frank C. Thames 2025

ISBNs: 9781009539586 (HB), 9781009430654 (PB), 9781009430616 (OC)
ISSNs: 2753-8117 (online), 2753-8109 (print)

Contents

1 Introduction — 1

2 Gendered Political Inequality and Life Expectancy in Conflict Countries — 21

3 Maternal Health Consequences — 35

4 Women's Experiences in Iraq at War: An In-Depth Look — 47

5 Concluding Thoughts — 62

References — 65

1 Introduction

How do women experience war? Two distinct threads of scholarship have developed exploring this question. First – women's standing in society and the occurrence of violence are related. Early feminist IR scholars like Enloe (1990, 1993) and Tickner et al. (1992) theorized the nature of this relationship and more quantitative scholars have provided empirical evidence. Melander (2016, p. 197) suggested that "the strongest pattern in civil war is probably the gendered nature," and Bakken and Buhaug (2021, p. 984) highlights the "near consensus finding that gender inequality is associated with increased risk of civil war."

Secondly, the consequences of war are also gendered. Civil conflict has significant, negative effects on maternal health (e.g., Kotsadam & Østby, 2019; Kottegoda, Samuel, & Emmanuel, 2008; Tamura et al., 2012; Urdal & Che, 2013).[1] Going a step further, public health scholars have explored the role that women's autonomy or empowerment plays in conflict outcomes related to maternal and infant health (e.g., Adjiwanou & LeGrand, 2014; Banda et al., 2017; Bloom, Wypij, & Gupta, 2001; Stephenson, Bartel, & Rubardt, 2012).

Far less attention has been paid to the interrelationship between these two processes. If gender affects both the occurrence of violence and the consequences of that violence, then it is essential for them to be considered together. Skeptics of gender equality as an important determinant of war and peace have expressed concern about endogeneity but rather than exploring the meaning of this inter-relationship, they have dismissed it. Our approach is different – as we put the connection front and center, both theoretically and methodologically. We place the focus on how gender inequality greatly increases the likelihood that states will experience armed conflict and the fact that women will suffer greater consequences in those conflicts that do occur. This is more an issue of sample selection rather than endogeneity. Women in Finland are less likely to experience harsh health conflict consequences. The comparatively small gender gap there makes it less likely that they will experience a war and make it more likely that women will receive excellent care should a conflict occur.

Gender is the most basic hierarchy in the human experience. Failure to recognize it as a power structure has implications for politics and, of course, our understanding of politics. Peterson (1992, p. 197) notes that we cannot fully

---

[1] The majority of these studies rely on micro-level survey data of individuals in single country case studies (e.g., Akseer et al., 2019; Chandrasekhar, Testayı Gebreselassie, & Jayaraman, 2010; Chi et al., 2015a; Das et al., 2020; Kotsadam & Østby, 2019; Mirzazada et al., 2020; Namasivayan et al., 2012; Nepal, Halla, & Stillman, 2023; Østby, Leiby, & Nordås, 2019; Torres & Urdinola, 2019).

understand real-world events based on solely on male-focused accounts that "render women and gender invisible." Moreover, as Sjoberg (2010) notes, representing the state as non-gendered does not make it so. Decisions about when to use force and as well as the decisions about how to invest in public good goods (for example, how much money should we allocate toward women's health programs) are a reflection of the gender attitudes and hierarchies in society.

In this Element, we discuss the research on the gender and war. Scholars have demonstrated that in societies where gender inequality is greater, armed conflict is more likely to occur (Caprioli, 2000, 2003). Once conflict has begun, women have a different, more indirect experience of armed conflict. After drawing this conclusion, we take the analysis an important step further. Where women's equality is low, conflict is more likely and women experience more negative consequences. If gender inequality affects both the causes and the consequences of war, then we need to consider the inherent connection between the two processes. If causes and consequences are clearly linked to each other as well as to gender political inequality, then efforts to prevent conflict as well as the humanitarian response to the consequences of war need to take gender into account.

Feminist View of Security

As a foundation of feminist security, it important to recognize that the word *gender* does not mean the biological differences between men and women because gender is culturally defined. Gender is a social construction and that social construction is one that denotes inequalities based on perceived differences between men and women (Scott, 1986; Tickner et al., 1992). All over the world, men are privileged and in a position of dominion over women (Tickner et al., 1992). Our understandings of gender create hierarchies based on perceptions of masculine and feminine characteristics (Sjoberg, 2010).

To fully understand the gendered causes and consequences of war, a feminist security lens is essential. Both the prosecution and study of armed conflict continue to be dominated by men (Sjoberg, 2010). Without a gendered lens, we miss the critical insights found in the feminist security literature. From this perspective, war is part of continuum of the violence experienced in everyday life rather than a separate and distinct event (Sjoberg, 2013). When militarized masculinity is widespread in society, any conflict is more likely to be met with violence (Enloe, 1993).

Using gender as a lens allows us to focus on power dynamics within a society. Taking the idea of gender hierarchy into consideration when we think about the causes and consequences of armed conflict, we must consider what

Sjoberg (2013) terms "relative vulnerabilities." In unequal societies where violence is already viewed as more acceptable, when conflict inevitably begins women are more vulnerable to its impacts because of their preexisting subordinate position in society. From this perspective, conflict encompasses violence in the household, and in society, as well as between states or rebel groups and governments. Violence has economic, social, and political consequences that are gendered because these consequences are filtered through the institutions and structures of society. A gendered approach enables scholars to focus on women's experiences and the ways in which those experiences reflect an unequal social position.

Gendered Causes of War

Mainstream scholarship on the causes of civil conflict has often highlighted greed and grievance (Collier & Hoeffler, 2004). Rebels are either victims fighting against religious or ethnic oppression, or they are brigands looking to seize loot like natural resources or other sources of wealth. While the greed versus grievance dichotomy is an oversimplification (Berdal, 2005), much of the popular discourse about civil wars focuses on these two explanations.

Traditional research on the causes of war fails to acknowledge that gender influences the occurrence of violence. Recent work on gender-blind approaches in political science (Forman-Rabinovici & Mandel, 2022; Paxton, 2000) demonstrates how not taking gender into account creates gaps in our understanding of political phenomena. For our purposes we wish to highlight the fact violence is a highly gendered practice.

Men and women play different roles in conflict. Who fights in wars is gendered as is how individuals are affected by the fighting (Bjarnegård et al., 2015). According to Goldstein (2001), less than 1% of warriors throughout history have been women, but biology alone cannot explain this imbalance. Under some circumstances, women perpetrate violence and can be highly effective fighters (Darden, Henshaw, & Szekely, 2019; Sjoberg & Gentry, 2011; Thomas & Bond, 2015; Wood & Thomas, 2017). The predominance of men in war is rooted in societal constructions and traditional gender norms that dictate that men defend the homeland and women maintain the home front. If anything, these gender role norms tend to be strengthen during wartime (Sjoberg, 2013).

Feminist scholars point out that gender is an essential aspect of violence in all societies because gender inequality exists in all societies (Caprioli, 2005). There are two primary explanations for why gender inequality might cause conflict. First is the essentialist argument – women are more peaceful by their natures. From this point of view, there are inherent differences in the attitudes of biological men and women (Goldstein, 2001; Melander, 2005). Given their preference for peaceful means of conflict resolution and their role as mothers, women are believed to be more averse to violence. In societies where political equality is greater, these peaceful tendencies of women have more influence on foreign policy decision-making. This preference for nonviolence may be born of upbringing or genetics (Bjarnegård & Melander, 2011; Melander, 2016).

In order to lessen violence in a society (or the international system or a household), the essentialist prescription would be to empower women. Women are less likely to use violence in daily interactions (Dahlum & Wig, 2020). Many studies of individual attitudes demonstrate that women prefer nonviolent methods of conflict resolution. When women are elected to public office, they can turn those preferences into policies that put fewer resources toward the military or increasing attention on social ills relating to underlying grievances that could turn violent (Melander, 2005).

This essentialist logic does not go unchallenged, however. By suggesting that *all* women, by their nature, prefer nonviolent methods of conflict resolution or are less likely to use force, many see this as reinforcing gender stereotypes (Mansbridge, 2005). Women vary in their political preferences as do men, and thus attributing gender as a cause of war seems at best incomplete.

The second explanation is more of a constructivist argument – meaning socially constructed norms about gender and gender roles influence how a society responds to conflict. Ideas about what is feminine and what is masculine affect attitudes toward violence. Men are expected to be warriors while women are caregivers, and in many cases, their upbringings reflect these differences (Melander, 2005). Men and boys are taught to be tough while women and girls are taught to be nurturing. Such stereotypes also highlight women's subordinate position in the societal hierarchy (Goldstein, 2001; Tickner et al., 1992). Boys who do not act tough and warlike are accused of being weak or girly, which is perceived as less than being manly and lessens social status.

Not only do traditional gender roles cement societal hierarchy, but they also legitimize violence as a man must do whatever it takes to defend the home and the honor of the women under his care. When men and women are more equal, violent and intolerant (masculine) methods of dealing with conflict are less dominant. From a constructivist point of view, the prescription for lessening violence would be to change the minds and perceptions of both men and women and thus shift societal norms.

These two explanations do not run counter to each other, and both may help us to understand the relationship between gender inequality and conflict (Caprioli, 2000, 2005; Goldstein, 2001; Melander, 2005; Tickner, 1997; Tickner et al., 1992). Both evolution and socio-economic conditions help us to understand why women tend to value peaceful solutions more than men (Melander, 2016). In egalitarian societies where women's preferences for interdependence and egalitarianism over pure competition are taken seriously (Welch & Hibbing, 1992), resources and health care are more likely to be available to all. Societies' constructed ideas about gender and gender roles also influence decision-making over how resources are allocated. Women's political empowerment and representation influences well-being outcomes for women and children, as well as for society as a whole (Bhalotra & Clots-Figueras, 2014). Without gender equality, national political cultures will be characterized by norms of violence. Those norms will, in turn, influence foreign policy and the way that the government responds to internal challenges. When inequality is high, the likelihood of violence will be too.

What Kind of Inequality?

Gender inequality exists everywhere, reflecting the gender hierarchies that exist in all societies (Webster, Chen, and Beardsley, 2019). Rich and poor countries, democracies as well as autocracies are all similar in this regard. What is less obvious is the fact that gender inequality can be a matter of life and death. Inequality has been linked to violence, ranging from domestic violence to war – both international wars (Caprioli, 2000, 2003; Hudson et al., 2009; Regan & Paskeviciute, 2003) and civil wars (Caprioli, 2005; Melander, 2005). Focusing on the causes of conflict, where gender inequality is high, tolerance for violence will be high, enhancing the ability of violent groups to mobilize support. How inequality has been conceptualized and measured, however, has varied.

Gender inequality can take several forms – economic, social, and political. Economic gender inequality includes unequal labor force participation and the existence of systematic pay gaps between men and women. The exclusion of women from financial decision-making in the household and unequal laws regarding property ownership and inheritance are additional examples. Social gender inequality make take the form of unequal access to education, forced marriages (often at young ages), lack of access to family planning services, and the absence of the right to divorce.

In this Element, we focus on political inequality. When women lack the right to vote or are under represented in government or lack standing in the judicial system, this is gendered political inequality. According to the World Economic Forum, political empowerment (or the degree to which women have influence in political and social spaces) is where the greatest gap exists worldwide between men and women, compared to educational attainment, economic opportunity, and health & survival (Zahidi, 2023). In their 2023 Global Gender

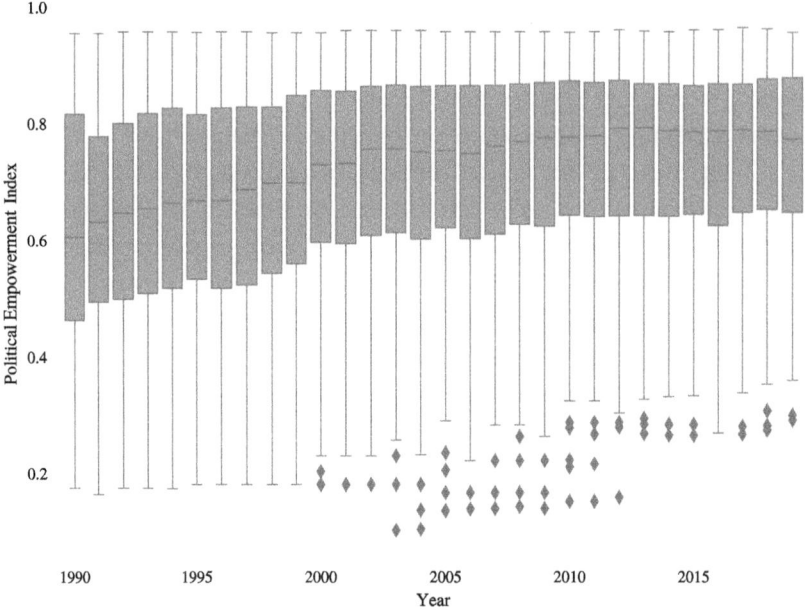

Figure 1 Political Empowerment Index, 1990–2019

Gap report, they posit that it will take 162 years for women to obtain political parity with men if the current rate of progress continues (Zahidi, 2023).

Figure 1 plots the *Political Empowerment Index* (Coppedge et al., 2023b; Pemstein et al., 2023) in 146 countries between 1990 and 2019. Political empowerment is defined as "a process of increasing capacity for women, leading to greater choice, agency, and participation in societal decision-making" (Coppedge et al., 2023a, p. 302).[2]

Figure 1 reveals several important patterns in women's political equality over time. First, the yearly median of the *Political Empowerment Index* has increased steadily over time, indicating that global empowerment has improved. Yet, the figure also reveals significant variation in the level of women's political empowerment. While equality maybe increasing globally, there remain a significant number of countries in which women maintain very limited political power. Thus, while the general record of women's political inequality has improved, we do see wide variation globally as well.

Because we are interested in the relationship between conflict and women's political empowerment, we next turn to see whether there's variation among

---

[2] The index is composed of three separate indices: the women's *Civil Liberties Index*, the women's *Civil Society Participation Index*, and the women's *Political Participation Index* (Coppedge et al., 2023a).

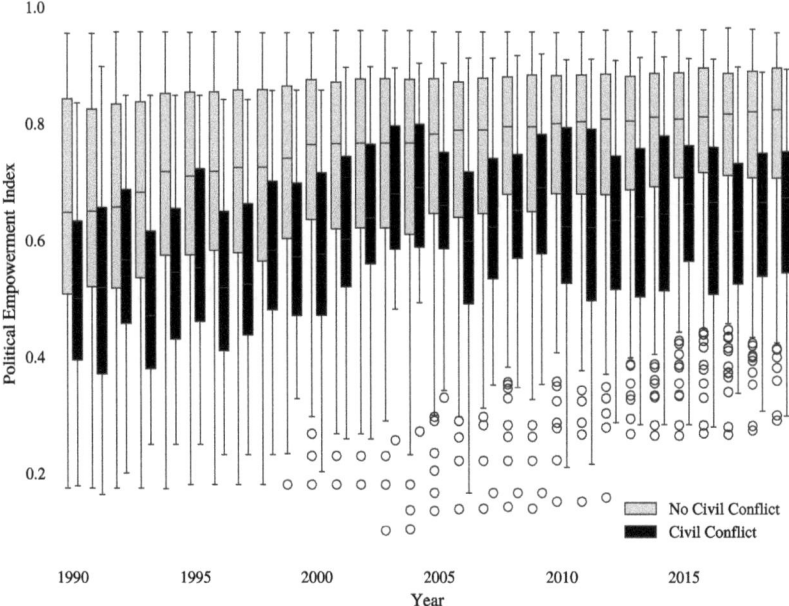

Figure 2 Political Empowerment Index by Conflict, 1990–2019

those countries experiencing civil conflict. The conflict variable indicates whether an intrastate conflict occurred in the country in a given year (Davies, Pettersson, & Öberg, 2022; Gleditsch et al., 2002). Figure 2 plots the *Political Empowerment Index* over time for countries with a civil conflict and those without. While, on average, women's political equality is lower in conflict countries, we still see significant variation in the level of inequality in conflict cases.

Previous studies have found that states with higher levels of political inequality are more likely to engage in both interstate (Caprioli, 2000, 2003; Hudson et al., 2009; Regan & Paskeviciute, 2003) and intrastate wars (Caprioli, 2005; Melander, 2005). Focusing on civil war, these states also experience greater rates of conflict recurrence (Demeritt, Nichols, & Kelly, 2014). In international conflicts, less equal states are more likely to escalate to violence (Caprioli & Boyer, 2001).

States with higher levels of women's political empowerment are less likely to employ violence than those with lower levels of gender equality at home. Violence toward women is a better predictor of a state's likelihood of participating in conflict than democracy, wealth, or prevalence of Islam (Hudson et al., 2009).

Given the empirical pattern shown in Figure 2 as well as the previous scholarship linking political inequality to violence, we believe that understanding how women's political inequality impacts health outcomes during times of conflict requires taking into account the fact that conflict is more likely in those countries with weak gender equality. The ways that women experience conflict are in part explained by the conditions in their home countries prior to the beginning of the conflict.

Gendered Consequences of War

Not only are the causes of conflict gendered, but the consequences of war are gendered as well. Less research has been done on this side of the coin, but as was the case with the research on gender and conflict onset, the work on gender and consequences has been done in isolation. The connection between the two has been under appreciated.

The mechanisms linking gender and the consequences of war are less clear. Scholars have identified a range of ways that conflict may affect women differently than men (discussed in detail in this Element), but there has been less consideration of how inequality – particularly political inequality – influences the degree of those impacts. Where women are already in a subordinate position in society, the effects of war will come down harder upon them.

The economic, health, and social consequences that occur beyond the battlefield are felt first by women and children (Sjoberg, 2012) and are not gender-neutral (Minoiu & Shemyakina, 2012). Women's well-being may be affected by three different mechanisms according to the conflict literature: the economic damage effect, the displacement effect, and the sexual violence effect. All three of these can be understood with greater clarity when we combine them with gender inequality.

Gendered Health Outcomes

Economic Effects

In the countries where wars are fought, productive members of society are killed, infrastructure is damaged or destroyed, and long-term damage is done to the economic, educational, and public health systems (Allen & Lektzian, 2013; Ghobarah, Huth, & Russett, 2004; Iqbal, 2006; Lai & Thyne, 2007). Critically, resources are diverted way from public programs that help women and children. This shift will be more dramatic in societies where women's representation is limited and masculine values prioritizing violence are reflected in policy choices.

The diminished quality of social programs in gender unequal societies will be magnified as the destruction associated with war degrades economies and economic potential going forward. These indirect costs can negatively impact a country's standard of health for many years following the termination of fighting. When the electrical grid is damaged, water purification and safety will deteriorate. Without clean water, healthy food, proper health care, or access to care, the health and well-being of women can quickly degrade. This is especially problematic in societies that failed to invest in women's health prior to the war.

Infrastructure is often targeted by combatants. By blowing up bridges and roads, combatants may hinder the movements of their adversaries, which has strategic benefits. Without roads and bridges, however, economic exchange is also hindered. Bringing goods to market becomes much more difficult. Hospitals may be blown up, and the roads and bridges needed to get to those hospitals destroyed. Fighting can decimate crops and agricultural land, compromising the food supply. In times of food scarcity, women and girls may be discriminated against in the distribution of food and medicine.

As fighting continues, resources that are needed to fund armed conflict are drawn disproportionately from public goods programs like health services, education, and policing many of which are highly beneficial to women. This is true for all societies, but where investment in public goods was lagging prior to the fighting, the impact will be greater. During civil war, states divert resources from productive sectors to violence, which causes society to lose twice over (Collier et al., 2003). Societies that fear attacks or violence typically prioritize security and de-prioritize policies that benefit women and their welfare (Tir & Bailey, 2017).

Where war spending is high in relation to state resources, the indirect social costs can become very large (Stewart & Fitzgerald, 2000). Civil wars reduce the productivity of the entire economy, damaging and disrupting the administrative and economic resources necessary to maintain previous levels of health expenditure (Ghobarah, Huth, and Russett, 2003, 2004). Diminished and diverted resources from public program negatively influence health outcomes over time.

When the shooting stops and combatants return home, these indirect effects of conflict often remain. Damage to croplands leads to food shortages, wrecked infrastructure curtails the transportation of goods and labor, a degraded health sector cannot tend to all the needs of the population – the list could go on. Underdevelopment is a frequent consequence of war. Resources are seldom immediately restored to their previous levels causing civilians to continue to suffer negative consequences during and after the fighting (Collier et al., 2003). Economic growth may be slowed, making it difficult to return to status quo public spending (Rehn & Sirleaf, 2002), particularly because governmental institutions are also weakened by conflict. Not only has money been allocated away from social programs during the conflict, even after the war ends it is clear that civil wars disrupt the state's ability to provide basic social services (Lai & Thyne, 2007).

The economic effects of conflict are also often indirect as resources needed to fund armed conflicts are drawn disproportionately from public goods programs like health services, education, and policing many of which are highly beneficial to women. These women face increased challenges of survival as clean water, food, fuel, electricity, and medicine are likely to be scarce (Ashford, 2008). In societies where women lack political rights and voice, these challenges are magnified. When women are in political leadership, they have the ability to advocate for funding for programs that benefit women and children. When they are absent, their priorities may fail to be considered. For example, child and maternal health initiatives may not be a legislative priority in a time of economic scarcity if there are no women to champion these programs.

Below the societal level, the costs of war can also be understood at the individual level. Women may be called upon to take on new roles in the household as men are called away to fight, required not only to provide domestic labor for the household but also to seek employment outside of the house in order to make ends meet. Women may also prioritize the health of their children under these circumstances, providing scarce medicine and food to young people rather than themselves.

Many women struggle with poverty (or deeper poverty) during war as husbands and sons who have been traditional breadwinners leave to fight. These women face increased challenges as clean water, food, fuel, electricity, and medicine are likely to be scarce (Ashford, 2008). Add to that diminished income, and women in many situations struggle to meet the basic survival needs of their families and themselves. In societies where women lack political rights or legal protections for basic rights like property ownership, this loss of income can be devastating. Poverty plays a tremendous role in shaping the lives that women lead and the rights and freedoms that they enjoy. Armed conflict increases poverty and worsens conditions behind the front lines.

Another way that gender inequality can affect the degree to which these indirect economic consequences has to do with the laws governing property rights. Engels (2010) acknowledges that women's subordinate position in society was driven in part by women's economic reliance on men as male-owned private property increased in the nineteenth century. Even today women lag behind in their rights to control property and to inherit. While the income associated with property is important, the issue is deeper.

Laws guaranteeing women's property rights consistently lag behind respect for men's property rights (World Bank, 2023). Without respect for property rights, women are unable to inherit or own land and remain entirely dependent on their relationships with male relatives, which further exacerbates vulnerabilities for domestic violence.

When husbands and fathers are killed in the fight, women may experience a diminished social position in some societies. The death of men in civil conflict also increases the percentage of female-headed households, which can introduce new challenges. Women may be unable to inherit land owned by their husbands and forced out of their homes.

The damage to social capital and social networks is often under appreciated as families are separated or destroyed. In developing countries, where families often constitute the primary form of insurance, the death of workers and displacement of individuals away from other family members and family land can have an adverse effect on health and security in the society even after the conflict ends (Blattman & Miguel, 2010). Thus, the effects of conflict may extend far into the future, well after armed conflict ceases.

When an economy experiences a major shock like a war or natural disaster, women are in a more vulnerable position as a result of their comparative poverty (True, 2012) and weaker legal protections (World Bank, 2023). The economic consequences of war hit women harder and more quickly, especially when political inequality is high. These are the countries where we observe wars happening – states that enact policies that encourage gender equality (and enforce them) are less likely to engage in conflict (Hudson, et al., 2012). War exacerbates the negative societal impacts due to gender political inequality.

Displacement Effects

Building on the previous discussion about how conflict creates vulnerability for women, especially when gender inequality is high, we now consider the way armed conflict displaces populations. The people most likely to need to flee their homes in search of safety are women and children.

In recent decades, most of the conflict driven displacement has been caused by civil rather than international wars (Lischer, 2007). Much like the stories of every woman in a war zone, every story of displacement is different but fear, persecution, scarcity, and human suffering are often hallmarks of these tales. The lucky among them are able to seek refuge with family or friends, but many others make their ways to camps looking for food, shelter, and a modicum of security (Norwegian Refugee Council, 2002). Others may take shelter in isolated countryside, unsure of whether or where to find assistance. Groups that have fled are already under strain and fear for their physical and economic well-being (Iqbal, 2010).

Women are more likely to be displaced or become refugees than men. Women are less likely to serve in armed conflict, and where gender equality is low, women have likely been exposed to violence at the hands of men – either in the broader society or in their own homes. Single-parent households led by women dominate the populations in refugee camps as women work to keep their children safe (Rehn & Sirleaf, 2002). Often health conditions in refugee or internally displaced persons (IDP) camps are poor, and reproductive health services are unlikely to be provided in these facilities as the primary concerns tend to be on essential needs like food, water, shelter, and the most basic health care (McGinn, 2000).

When displaced individuals seek outside assistance, their concerns about well-being may not be completely alleviated. In fact, they are likely just shifted in another direction. Displaced persons face a number of risks, including a greater chance of disease transmission. The makeshift nature of refugee camps make them easy breeding grounds for illness. In addition, these camps are often in remote locations without access to health care and basic necessities such as clean water (Gleick, 1993; Hoddie & Smith, 2009). Refugees and displaced persons are not evenly distributed across a country (Salehyan & Gleditsch, 2006), and thus, the health effects may not be evenly distributed. Getting supplies to these areas can be greatly complicated by on-going fighting.

Refugee camps often lack of consistent access to clean water, which degrades hygiene and increases the risk of infectious diseases (Ghobarah, Huth, & Russett, 2004; Gleick, 1993). The lack of water and firewood (or other sources of heat for cooking food) can also hinder the preparation nutritious food, leading to poor health and malnutrition (Toole & Waldman, 1993). Without water and nutritious food, refugee families often find themselves in a cycle of poor health and malnutrition (Toole & Waldman, 1993).

Displaced persons face a greater chance of disease transmission. The makeshift nature of refugee camps makes them easy breeding grounds for illness. In addition, these camps are often in remote locations and lack access to health care (Hoddie & Smith, 2009). For example, Montalvo and Reynal-Querol (2007) finds that for every 1,000 refugees that arrive in a country, an additional 2,700 cases of malaria occur in that receiving country. Congested camps in Ethiopia in the late 1980s had a huge outbreak of typhus, and dysentery and cholera devastated Rwandan refugees in 1994 (World Health Organization, 2003). Toole (1997) reports mortality rates that are up to 100 times higher in these camps than the normal rates in the affected countries.

While refugees often face harsh health conditions, internally displaced people may suffer even more than refugees as their situations are often beyond the reach of international aid agencies (Toole & Waldman, 1993). According to the Office of the High Commissioner on Human Rights, "internally displaced persons (also known as IDPs) are persons or groups of persons who have been forced or obliged to flee or to leave their homes or places of habitual residence, in particular as a result of or in order to avoid the effects of armed conflict, situations of generalized violence, violations of human rights or natural or human-made disasters, and who have not crossed an internationally recognized border" (UNHCR, n.d.).

Displacement also has longer-term consequences as the population movements cause the disruption or destruction of social networks and social capital (Kondylis, 2010). This can be particularly harmful in less developed countries where extended family networks are often the primary mechanism for insurance (Blattman & Miguel, 2010). All of these challenges – reduced economic circumstances, physical threats, and the difficulties of keeping a family together – begin to wear on women who face high levels of anxiety and stress while living in these camps. Amowitz, Heisler, and Iacopino (2003) found high rates of depression among displaced Afghani women living in Pakistan.

Economic assets will likely be lost and resettlement can be challenging, which again echoes the unique struggles women face due to the indirect economic costs of war. Displacement can lead to a vicious cycle of household poverty that is difficult to escape (Buvinic et al., 2013), especially in areas where property rights for women are limited. In Cote d'Ivoire where the primary wealth is held in land, the customary system of land ownership discriminates against women making it difficult or in some places impossible for women to own land (UN Women, 2020). For many women who were displaced by conflict there, when they returned home their claims to family land was either ignored or ruled against. Displaced populations often suffer physically, economically, and emotionally. Laws that reinforce gendered economic inequality exacerbate this suffering. If women lack standing in court or equal protection under the law, their efforts to rebuild their lives after war will be much more challenging than those of their male counterparts.

Gender-Based Violence Effects

Conflict-related sexual violence has some of the most obvious gendered consequences. Gender-based violence increases not only at the hands of enemies but also in the form of domestic abuse during conflict (True, 2012). While men can also be the victims of such violence during conflict and women can also be perpetrators (Gentry & Sjoberg, 2015; Sjoberg & Gentry, 2007, 2011), the victims are much more likely to be women (Cohen, 2013). Violence against women generally increases with the decline of law and order in conflict states. Under such conditions, women's security may be threatened both inside and outside of their homes as the whole of society is ruled by aggression and violence

(Rehn & Sirleaf, 2002). Militarization changes societies and increases violence (Enloe, 2010). Conflict leads to a degrading of social norms about what is appropriate behavior, and more risk-taking occurs, which can have devastating effects on women. This type of violence has been employed as a weapon of war and of ethnic cleansing in civil conflicts around the world (Carpenter, 2006; Cohen, 2013; Wood, 2009).

Research suggests that some degree of sexual violence occurs in all conflicts, but that there is a great deal of variation in the type and extent (Cohen & Nordås, 2014; Wood, 2009). This type of violence has been employed as a weapon of war and of ethnic cleansing in civil conflicts around the world (Carpenter, 2006; Cohen, 2013; Wood, 2006).

The International Criminal Court (ICC) defines sexual violence as "an act of a sexual nature against one or more persons or caused such person or persons to engage in an act of a sexual nature by force, or by threat of force or coercion, such as that caused by fear of violence, duress, detention, psychological oppression or abuse of power, against such person or persons or another person, or by taking advantage of a coercive environment or such person's or persons' incapacity to give genuine consent" (Article 7(1)(g)-6) (International Criminal Court, 2011). This includes rape, sexual slavery, forced prostitution, forced pregnancy, and forced sterilization/abortion.[3] Cohen (2013) suggests that while wartime rape may be devastating for both the victims and the perpetrators, it should be considered independently from lethal uses of force, building on Wood (2009) which notes that patterns of rape are distinct from those associated with homicide and displacement in war. In addition, rape is often utilized as the alternative for mass killings of male populations, especially in circumstances of ethnic conflict.

While rape may be used during war either strategically or opportunistically, intimate partner violence also increases greatly both during and after conflict (Mooney, 2005). When gender inequality is high, domestic violence is already occurring at a higher rate than in more equal societies. While research has put the focus on mass sexual violence like strategic rape, these acts as part of a broader range of gender-based violence (True, 2012). Violence against women more generally increases with the decline of law and order in conflict states. Under such conditions, women's security may be threatened both inside and outside of their homes as the whole of society is ruled by aggression and violence (Rehn & Sirleaf, 2002). Militarization changes societies and increases violence (Enloe, 2010). Conflict leads to a degrading of social norms about

---

[3] The definition of sexual violence is gender neutral. Men can also be victims of this type of violence and women can also be perpetrators.

what is appropriate behavior, and more risk-taking occurs. Both domestic violence and sexual abuse in the home also increase.

Women can be sexually assaulted as a means of humiliating their families (Rehn & Sirleaf, 2002). Civilian terror is a tactic of war, one that is being employed more frequently in modern conflict. Women may also feel obligated to trade sex for protection from local rebel leaders. Gender-based violence increases not only at the hands of enemies, but also in the form of domestic abuse during conflict (True, 2012). During civil war, gender stereotypes are not only reinforced but often increase in strength (Goldstein, 2001). Sexual violence is more likely when the stereotypes reinforce traditional gender roles.

An additional issue related to sexual violence as well as women's health is the challenge of HIV/AIDS. The head of UNAIDS has noted that "conflict and HIV are entangled as twin evils" (quoted in Elbe (2002, p. 160)). The violent nature of these attacks can also increase the likelihood of infection (Singer, 2002). In Rwanda and the Democratic Republic of Congo, soldiers expressed a stated intention of transmitting the disease through rape (UNAIDS, 2000). While Spiegel (2004) has demonstrated that the link between conflict and HIV prevalence is complex, women and displaced persons are often a greater risk for infection in war torn countries. Women are vulnerable due to their physiological and social disadvantages. Treatment and appropriate drugs for many sexually transmitted diseases are relatively common, but medical attention and medication are often difficult to obtain in conflict states.

Connecting these issues to the challenges of displacement, women in refugee camps often find that they need to be constantly vigilant because of the increased threat of sexual violence to themselves and their children (Sjoberg, 2013). Women may also have to guard against those who would attempt to recruit their children into the fighting. These women are also often separated from their extended families, which can complicate the process of returning or rebuilding after displacement.

Sexual violence against women often come with a stigma or results in the blaming of the victim. When women lack a political voice and feel unprotected by the legal system, sexual violence may already be a regular occurrence even before armed conflict breaks out. When the war begins, this societal pattern will be intensified. The wartime challenges that women face are both a result and a reflection of the position of women in peacetime (True, 2012).

Women's Health Outcomes during Conflict

In the previous sections, we have laid out three ways that armed conflict could negatively impact the health of women in distinct ways, but we also know

Table 1 First differences *Conflict* variable, models 1.1. and 1.2

Model	Dependent Variable	5%	50%	95%
1.1	Female Life Expectancy	−0.834	−0.643	−0.460
1.2	ln(MMR)	0.001	0.025	0.049

Note: Table reports the posterior median and 90% Credibility Intervals.

that health policies created during peace time have gendered consequences. To demonstrate the difference between the health outcomes that women experience in countries at peace versus those in countries at war, we constructed a dataset of 146 countries between 1990 and 2019. As we will do in Sections 2 and 3, we focus here on two major measures of women's health – *Female Life Expectancy*, which measures life expectancy at birth for women measured in years (Teorell et al., 2023; World Bank, 2022) and the natural log of the maternal mortality rate, *ln(MMR)* (World Health Organization, 2023). We use a dichotomous variable measuring the presence of *Civil Conflict* (Davies, Pettersson, & Öberg, 2022; Gleditsch et al., 2002). We include a measure of gendered political inequality by including the women's *Political Empowerment Index*, which measures women's political empowerment (Coppedge et al., 2023b; Pemstein et al., 2023).

Table 1 includes the first differences of the *Conflict* variable from two Bayesian hierarchical linear models of women's health outcomes – *Female Life Expectancy* and *ln(MMR)*.[4] The results clearly show that the presence of a conflict, in comparison to those countries without a civil conflict, undermines women's health outcomes. The presence of a civil conflict decreases *Female Life Expectancy* by 0.643 years. *Conflict* increases the *ln(MMR)* by 0.025, which represents a 2.5% increase in the maternal mortality rate. Thus, while women may face obstacles to health care in countries at peace, we find evidence that the presence of civil conflict worsens outcomes. Along with the theoretical discussion earlier, we take this as our jumping off point for turning our focus to the inter related impacts of political inequality on both the causes and consequences of war. Where women lack political agency, their health suffers. When conflict occurs in those countries, the problems are magnified.

Making the Connections

Our review of the literature on women and conflict leads to a critical conclusion – gender, and, more specifically, the political inequalities defined

---

[4] The appendix contains discussion of the models, the control variables, and tables of detailed estimates.

by gendered hierarchiess impact both the causes and consequences of war. First, the evidence clearly demonstrates that the unequal treatment of women increases the probability of conflict. Second, the impact of war on women is significant, due to their unequal status in society. The impact of gender hierarchies is cemented into place by political inequality. Despite the fact that women suffer fewer combat deaths, they are far more likely to suffer the indirect consequences of war. This is an effect of the fact that violence is far more likely in gender unequal societies. These processes are inextricably linked.

In today's conflicts, women face substantial morbidity and mortality consequences (Bendavid et al., 2021), in large part because of their unequal positions before and during conflict. Where women lack a political voice, gender inequalities of all types (political, economic, and social) will lead to heightened consequences. When women are under represented in government and discriminated against in political institutions like the judicial system, they will suffer from reduced social safety nets, damaged infrastructure, weakened economies, insecurities associated with displacement, and sexual violence – all of which can lead to increased mortality and morbidity. Evidence suggests that women's descriptive representation leads to improved women's health outcomes (Mechkova & Edgell, 2023).

Recognizing this fact leads us to the expectation that both the presence and impact of conflict will depend, in part, on the level of gender inequality in a society. While women in nearly every country are poorer than men and have a more limited voice in politics, the inequality between men and women varies across countries. Existing research on the position of women in different societies finds strong evidence that states vary across key indicators such as the percentage of women in the legislature (Schwindt-Bayer & Squire, 2014), maternal mortality rate (Banda et al., 2017), and access to education (Zahidi, 2023), among others. If gendered inequality explains the cause and consequences of war, then we would expect that variation in inequality will lead to variation in both the presence and consequence of war. Conflict typically occurs in countries where women's status is lower compared to men. As a result, the women's health consequences from war are significant because we are only observing them in states where women are in a position of political weakness. They lack voices in legislative bodies and the policies that have been created by those legislatures have not been centered on their needs.

Recognizing that women's political equality affects both the likelihood and consequences of civil conflict complicates how we measure the effects of civil conflict on women's health. Unless dealt with this, our empirical analysis could suffer from selection bias. Selection bias arises when variables affect not on the creation of the sample but also the outcomes in which we are interested (Böhmelt & Spilker, 2020; Sartori, 2003). The presence of selection bias could lead to biased estimations from our outcome equations (Heckman, 1979). The concern is important enough that issues of selection bias are common in the broader IR scholarship (Böhmelt & Spilker, 2020; Clayton & Dorussen, 2021; Dorussen, Böhmelt, & Clayton, 2022).

We argue that selection bias likely affects our analysis based on the existing theoretical literature for several reasons. There could be unmeasured factors that influence both the likelihood of conflict and women's health outcomes. Countries that have weak gender equality are more likely to suffer not only from conflict but also from weak women's health outcomes. Thus, to accurately understand the effects of civil conflict on women's health, we need to take into account the issue of selection bias.

To test our argument about the inter relationship between gender inequality and conflict, we use two different empirical strategies. First, we employ regression analysis using our cross-sectional time-series dataset of global civil conflicts between 1990 and 2019. For this analysis, we utilize a two-stage Bayesian Heckman selection model.[5]

Second, we undertake a case-study of Iraq in the early twenty-first century. We believe Iraq offers an interesting testing ground for our theory because of differences between the laws governing women's political empowerment in south and central Iraq versus the Kurdish Regional Government. Women in the Kurdish region have been serving in the regional parliament since 1992, and in 2012, they held nearly one third of the seats. Comparing women's health outcomes across governorates allows us to examine whether improvements in women's social position increase the uptake of services that lessen maternal mortality.

Plan for the Element

In this Element, we empirically test the implications of the sample selection that results from gender inequality. In the places where wars occur, women are vulnerable and we expect that as that vulnerability increases, women will suffer greater negative health and well-being effects from war.

In Section 2, we focus on how armed conflict affects female life expectancy. Several previous studies have examined whether conflict is related to changes

---

[5] Our estimator is based on the classical two-stage Heckman selection model which pairs a probit model with a linear model (Böhmelt & Spilker, 2020). We do, however, estimate hierarchical models to take into account the different error variances between countries. We adopt Bayesian inference methods for our selection models.

in female life expectancy (e.g., Li & Wen, 2005; Plümper & Neumayer, 2006), but they fail to acknowledge how women's position in society affects the likelihood of violence that causes these negative outcomes. In Section 3, we examine maternal mortality rates. As with life expectancy, maternal mortality rates have been examined in other studies of conflict effects (e.g., Kotsadam & Østby, 2019; Kottegoda, Samuel, & Emmanuel, 2008; Tamura et al., 2012; Urdal & Che, 2013), but again, none of these studies regarding female life expectancy or maternal health consider the connection between causes and consequences of conflict.

While female life expectancy and maternal mortality (MMR) are related, they have different underlying mechanisms. In order to predict levels of maternal mortality in a society, population characteristics such as size, poverty rates, and percentage of those living in cities are important indicators. When we think about life expectancy, on the other hand, conflict characteristics like the length of the war and its intensity as well as the regime type of the conflict state are important predictors. Because different societal forces are driving these outcomes, we think it is important to consider how the inter relationship between conflict and gender inequality might affect them.

Additionally, maternal mortality is in and of itself gendered in nature. In unequal societies, policies may exist that do not prioritize maternal health. Life expectancy, on the other hand, is not. Even in unequal societies, investments in programs that enhance men's health could lead to improvements in life expectancy, even if women have a more difficult time accessing them.

In Section 4, we take an in-depth look at how decades of violence in Iraq have affected women. The type of conflict has varied over time and location within the country as has the intensity. Examining the experiences of Iraqi women allows us to pinpoint how exposure to violence affects women's well-being. In addition, the laws regarding women's political empowerment are not the same across the whole state of Iraq. The Kurdish Regional Government has had the opportunity since 1991 to pass distinct laws, differences have emerged. In this section, we examine whether or not these policy differences have an impact on women's well-being.

Finally, in Section 5, we briefly review our findings, noting their importance. Moreover, we expand on the policy implications of our results. If anything, our analysis highlights the importance of gendered political inequality in reducing both the incidence of civil conflicts and its consequences as well. These findings strengthen the international community's case for bringing more women into peace processes and the political systems that created or revised as a result of armed conflict.

Appendix

The estimates reported in figure 1 are taken from the models reported in Tables 2 and 3. We estimated both models using a Bayesian hierarchical-linear model with random intercepts for individual countries. We estimated 10,000 iterations with a burn-in of 5,000 iterations for each model. The diagnostics, included in the detailed results, indicate that each model converged.

For both models, we included our *Conflict* dummy variable to estimate the effects of civil conflict on health outcomes (Davies, Pettersson, & Öberg, 2022; Gleditsch et al., 2002). In model 1.1, Table 2, the dependent variable is *Female Life Expectancy* (Teorell et al., 2023; World Bank, 2022). In model 1.2, Table 3, we measured women's health outcomes with the natural log of the maternal mortality rate *ln(MMR)*. Again, our measure for women's political equality was taken from V-Dem–*Political Empowerment Index*, which measures women's political empowerment (Coppedge et al., 2023b; Pemstein et al., 2023).

We include a set of control variables typical for models of female life expectancy, model 1.1. We control for differences in levels of democracy by including *Polyarchy* (Coppedge et al., 2023b; Pemstein et al., 2023). Life expectancy may vary by wealth, so we include the natural log of GDP per capita, *Ln(GDP PC)* (Bolt & van Zanden, 2020; Teorell et al., 2023). We control for differences

Table 2 Detailed parameter estimates, Model 1.1

Parameter	5%	50%	95%	$\hat{R}$
Conflict	−0.834	−0.643	−0.460	1.001
Political Empowerment Index	6.413	7.505	8.633	1.001
Polyarchy	−2.105	−1.406	−0.659	1.001
Ln(GDP PC)	4.240	4.490	4.729	1.000
Ln(Population)	6.679	7.099	7.516	1.004
% AIDS Prevalence Adults	−0.852	−0.817	−0.781	1.001
Duration	0.001	0.002	0.002	1.001
% Rural	−0.147	−0.129	−0.112	1.001
% Population Growth	0.208	0.254	0.301	1.000
Intercept	69.721	70.843	72.097	1.030
σ_{beta}	2.260	2.868	3.636	1.000
σ_y	1.730	1.762	1.797	1.000
$\sigma_{country}$	8.284	8.928	9.642	1.001
N	3955			

Note: Table reports the posterior coefficient and parameter estimates.

Table 3 Detailed parameter estimates, model 1.2

Parameter	5%	50%	95%	$\widehat{R}$
Conflict	0.000	0.025	0.049	1.002
Political Empowerment Index	−0.864	−0.740	−0.618	1.000
Ln(GDP PC)	−0.922	−0.894	−0.865	1.001
Ln(Population)	−0.352	−0.306	−0.256	1.011
% AIDS Prevalence Adults	0.025	0.030	0.034	1.000
% Rural	0.005	0.007	0.009	1.003
Intercept	4.072	4.195	4.310	1.030
σ_{beta}	0.354	0.554	0.977	1.000
σ_y	0.227	0.231	0.235	1.001
$\sigma_{country}$	0.845	0.934	1.039	1.002
N	3955			

Note: Table reports the posterior coefficient and parameter estimates.

in population with the natural log of population *ln(Population)* (Teorell et al., 2023; World Bank, 2022). Variation in AIDS prevalence may lead to differences in female life expectancy; consequently, we include the *% AIDS Prevalence Adults* to control for greater death rates due to HIV (UN AIDS, 2023). Regime stability may matter, so we code all observations with the duration of the current regime in years *Duration* (Coppedge et al., 2023b; Pemstein et al., 2023). Differences in urban and rural areas may matter so we include the percentage of the population living in rural areas, *% Rural Population* (Teorell et al., 2023; World Bank, 2022). Finally, we include the rate of population growth, *% Population Growth* (Teorell et al., 2023; World Bank, 2022).

We utilize a similar set of controls of our model of *ln(MMR)*, model 1.2 in Table 3. We include the *Ln(GDP PC)*, *% Rural*, *% AIDS Prevalence Adults*, and *ln(Population)* (Bolt & van Zanden, 2020; Teorell et al., 2023; UN AIDS, 2023).

2 Gendered Political Inequality and Life Expectancy in Conflict Countries

In this section, we begin our examination of the gendered health consequences of war. Estimating the effect of conflict on life expectancy is a common method of estimating the societal impacts of war (e.g., Gates et al., 2012; Plümper & Neumayer, 2006). If the expectation is that conflict has a deleterious effect on women's health, then this is an obvious first place to look.

Women's life expectancy in all countries – regardless of whether or not they experience conflict – is influenced by their position in society. Access to health care and education as well as income levels and social safety nets all influence life expectancy and are influenced by gender equality. Life expectancy for women will be lower where women's positions in society are lower. This must be taken into account when examining the life expectancy consequences of conflict for women. Women in conflict societies already have lower rates of life expectancy when the first shot is fired compared to their counterparts in more peaceful societies.

Life Expectancy and Political Equality

Life expectancy at birth is understood to be a good indicator of overall population health and is shaped by various factors, many of which are influenced by gender (Pinho-Gomes, Peters, & Woodward, 2023). Does the level of gendered political inequality impact women's life expectancy? Based on the existing research, there is strong evidence to believe that it does. Because of the traditional gender hierarchies around the world, men in all countries, regardless of income level, have more control over their lives (UNDP, 2018). They have greater access to political power, economic resources, and the political processes by which resource allocation decisions are made. Where women lack political agency, their life expectancy may be lower.

Policies that promote gender equality should improve female life expectancy (Mateos et al., 2022). Focusing on political equality, government policies on health can be influenced by the presence (or absence) of women in the legislature and women's political engagement and empowerment. Women are more committed to social issues (Karam & Lovenduski, 2005; Reingold, 2003; Welch, 1985). Women's representation increases social spending (Bolzendahl & Brooks, 2007), and an increase in the share of women in cabinet is associated with an increase in public health spending (Mavisakalyan, 2014). In developing countries where women make up at least 20% of the lower house of the legislature, health outcomes like measles immunization, DPT immunizations, and infant and child morality all improve, and incremental increases in women's representation lead to the greatest improvement in socially and economically disadvantaged countries (Swiss, Fallon, & Burgos, 2012).

Female legislators often prioritize women's health once they take office. In Argentina, female legislators introduced 80% more pieces of legislation on reproductive rights than their male counterparts (Franceschet & Piscopo, 2008). Beyond introducing legislation regarding women's health, Westfall and

Chantiles (2016) shows that women's health outcomes are better in countries where women's representation is higher, particularly as a result of gender quotas.

With greater political engagement by educated women, investment specifically in women's health increases. In the next section, we discuss maternal health in greater detail, but investment in women's health results in more midwives (Van Lerberghe et al., 2014), more contraception (Bentley & Kavanagh, 2008), and lower fertility rates (Beer, 2009; Fuse & Crenshaw, 2006), all of which improve female life expectancy.

Women's Life Expectancy in Conflict Societies

Now we turn to examining the impact of conflict on women's life expectancy. Several existing studies suggest that on balance that the impact of civil conflict is disproportionately felt by women (Li & Wen, 2005; Plümper & Neumayer, 2006; Rehn & Sirleaf, 2002). The impact may vary over time as the health effects of conflict for men may be more concentrated in the short- and medium-term, while the effects for women have the potential to be longer-term (Ghobarah, Huth, & Russett, 2003). Gates et al. (2010) find a deleterious effect in fragile states, but it is unclear whether the conflict or state fragility is the driving factor. In a more recent study, Hoddie and Smith (2009) find that the health costs of conflict for women vary by age cohort. With a more refined estimation strategy, we attempt to clarify relationship found in some, but not all, previous studies.

Conflict may also indirectly affect well-being by decreasing the availability of education, particularly to women and girls (Buvinić, Das Gupta, & Shemyakina, 2014; Guha-Sapir & D'Aoust, 2011; Shemyakina, 2011). While improvements in female literacy lead to improved health and well-being, the inverse is also true. National literacy rates also correspond to life expectancy with better-educated populations enjoying longer lives (Kabir, 2008). These indirect economic consequences of war, including the destruction of infrastructure, degraded public education, and increased poverty, are all likely to hit women hard and to negatively impact women's health. The impact of all of these consequences will be magnified in countries where women lack equal political, social, and economic access.

As the economic costs rise and civilian infrastructure is destroyed, women may lack the ability to access life saving health care. Funding for public health services may be cut or shifted to military efforts, thus also diminishing care. Women are more likely to depend on such services. Women's health services are also more likely to be on the budgetary chopping block in societies where women's political voices are muted.

When populations are displaced, the ability to access care is disrupted. Refugee camps have notoriously poor sanitation, and communicable disease often runs rampant. Women dominate the populations of such camps. Displaced women and girls face greater challenges to their well-being than their male counter-parts.

In addition, sexual violence and sexually transmitted disease will likely increase, which can also have an negative impact on women's life expectancy. This size of this effect will be greater in societies where women lack political voice and violence against women is seen as more acceptable.

Based on the discussion earlier, we expect that the likelihood of conflict will depend on gendered political equality, which should in turn influence the negative consequences on women's health. Because more unequal states are more likely to experience conflict, women in conflict states are more likely to experience larger, negative impacts on life expectancy than in those societies that are more equal. Consequently, we hypothesize that:

Hypothesis 2.1: *In conflict countries, as women's political empowerment decreases, women's life expectancy will decrease.*

Measuring the Impact of Conflict on Life Expectancy

We test our hypotheses using a dataset of 145 countries between 1990 and 2019. The unit of analysis is country-year. As mentioned previously, we utilize a two-stage Bayesian Heckman selection model to control for the potential selection effects on conflict consequences.[6] We include random intercepts at the country level to control for differences in variance estimates by country. We mean center all of our model continuous covariates to ease convergence.[7] The ρ parameters for models 2.1–2.5 are statistically significant and negatively correlated, varying between −0.68 and −0.24; these results support our decision to use a selection model.[8] For all second-stage covariates, which were included in the first stage, we adjust the coefficients to take into account their impact on the probability of conflict (Sweeney, 2003).

Our first stage models conflict. Our dependent variable, *Conflict*, indicates whether an intrastate conflict occurred in the country in a given year (Davies, Pettersson, & Öberg, 2022; Gleditsch et al., 2002). In the second stage, our

---

[6] Our model is simply a Bayesian adaptation of the class two-stage Heckmkan selection model.
[7] For each model, we estimate four chains with 10,000 iterations each and a burn-in of 5,000 iterations. Model diagnostics indicate that all parameter estimates converged. All models were estimated in PyStan 3.7 (Riddell, Hartikainen, & Carter, 2021); the analyses were conducted using ArviZ 0.15.1 (Kumar et al., 2019).
[8] Detailed parameter estimates are located in the appendix to this section.

dependent variable is *Female Life Expectancy*, which measures life expectancy at birth for women measured in years (Teorell et al., 2023; World Bank, 2022).

We measure women's political empowerment using a series of variables taken from the V-Dem 13 dataset (Coppedge et al., 2023b; Pemstein et al., 2023). Model 2.1 uses the women's *Political Empowerment Index* (Coppedge et al., 2023a). More equal societies will have greater values on the women's *Political Empowerment Index*, while more unequal societies will have lower values. The index is composed of three separate indices–the women's *Civil Liberties Index* (model 2.2), the women's *Civil Society Participation Index* (model 2.3), and the women's *Political Participation Index* (model 2.4) (Coppedge et al., 2023a). It is possible that the impact of these different elements of the empowerment index will have different effects on the causes and consequences of conflict; therefore, we run models using these three indices separately. Finally, in model 2.5, we include *% Women in the Legislature*, which measures the percentage of women in the lower chamber of the legislature (Coppedge et al., 2023a). Based on our argument, we expect each of these measures to be negatively correlated with *Conflict*, but positively correlated with *Female Life Expectancy*.

We include several control variables in our first stage. First, we control for differences in the level of economic development, using the natural log of GDP per capita, *ln(GDP PC)* (Bolt & van Zanden, 2020; Teorell et al., 2023). Previous research finds that civil conflict is more common in poorer countries (Gates et al., 2012; Theisen, 2008). Second, we include the natural log of population, *ln(Population)*, to control for differences in population size (Teorell et al., 2023; World Bank, 2022). Civil conflict is more likely as population increases (Theisen, 2008). Third, we control for ethnic diversity by including a measure of ethnic fractionalization –*Ethnic Frac.* (Collier & Hoeffler, 2002; Fearon, 2003; Teorell et al., 2023). Fourth, we include the natural log of each country's mountainous terrain, *ln(Mountain Terrain)*, to control for the impact of a country's terrain on conflict (Miller, 2022). Research shows that mountainous terrain is more favorable for rebel groups, increasing the probability of civil conflict (Bohara, Mitchell, & Nepal, 2006; Carter, Shaver, & Wright, 2019; Hendrix, 2011). Fifth, we code each country/year with its level of democracy based on the V-Dem *Polyarchy* index (Coppedge et al., 2023b; Pemstein et al., 2023). Civil conflicts are more common in less democratic countries (Theisen, 2008). Fourth, we measure the number of neighboring states that are experiencing conflict, *N Neighbor Conflicts* as well (Miller, 2022). Previous work finds that civil conflict often spreads to neighboring countries (Fearon & Laitin, 2003; Gibler & Miller, 2014; Nunn & Puga, 2012; Riley, DeGloria, & Elliot, 1999). Finally, we include a dummy variable indicating whether there was a previous conflict in the country, *Previous Conflict*, for each observation (Davies, Pettersson, & Öberg, 2022; Gleditsch et al., 2002).

The second stages of our models include similar control variables. First, we include controls for democracy, *Polyarchy* (Coppedge et al., 2023b; Pemstein et al., 2023). Regime type may impact the quality of life; therefore, it could influence life expectancy (Plümper & Neumayer, 2006). Second, we control for wealth by including the *Ln(GDP PC)* (Bolt & van Zanden, 2020; Teorell et al., 2023). Those in wealthier countries have more resources and better health infrastructures; therefore, we expect female life expectancy to depend on a countries wealth (Baum & Lake, 2003; Bergh & Nilsson, 2010; Kennelly, O'Shea, & Garvey, 2003; Plümper & Neumayer, 2006). Third, we control for population by including *ln(Population)* (Teorell et al., 2023; World Bank, 2022). The provision of health resources could be dependent upon the size of the population (Baum & Lake, 2003). Fourth, we include the *% AIDS Prevalence Adults* to control for greater death rates due to HIV (UN AIDS, 2023). AIDS prevalence has been found to limit life expectancy (Plümper & Neumayer, 2006). Fifth, we code all observations with the duration of the current regime, *Duration* (Coppedge et al., 2023b; Pemstein et al., 2023). More durable regimes may provide a more stable environment, improving health outcomes (Plümper & Neumayer, 2006). Sixth, we include the percentage of the population living in rural areas, *% Rural Population* (Teorell et al., 2023; World Bank, 2022). Urban areas often contain better health infrastructure than do rural ones (Bergh & Nilsson, 2010; Kotsadam & Østby, 2019; Torres & Urdinola, 2019; Urdal & Che, 2013). Finally, we include the rate of population growth, *% Population Growth* (Teorell et al., 2023; World Bank, 2022). Rapid population growth can pose a strain on state resources, potentially limiting resources for health care.

To begin our analysis, we examine the results of the first stages of our models (2.1 through 2.5) in order to test hypothesis 2.1. In Figure 3, we plot the posterior medians and 90% credibility intervals of the first differences for all covariates.[9] For continuous variables, the first differences represent the change in the probability of conflict if we increase the value of each variable from one standard deviation below its mean to one standard deviation above its mean. For dummy variables, the first differences are the change in the probability of conflict if we increase the value of the variable from 0 to 1.

---

[9] All figures in this section were created using the Seaborn data visualization library (Waskom, 2021).

Conflict and Maternal Health

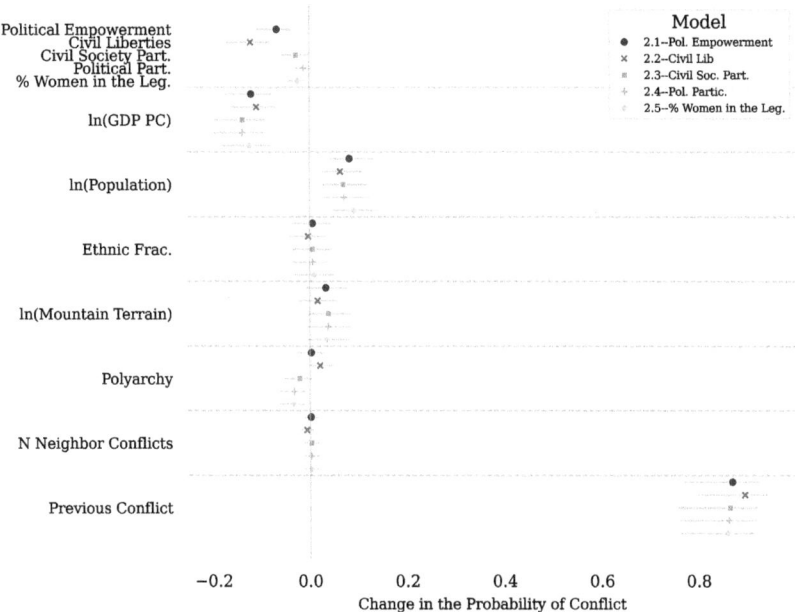

Figure 3 Conflict first differences, models 2.1–2.5
Note: Posterior Medians and 90% Cr. Int.

The estimates presented in Figure 3 provide support for hypothesis 2.1 – the probability of conflict decreases as women's political equality increases. Increasing equality on four of our five covariates (*Political Empowerment Index*, *Civil Liberties Index*, *Civil Society Participation Index*, and *% Women in the Legislature*) reduces the probability of conflict between 1.2% (*% Women in the Legislature* and 12.1% (*Civil Liberties Index*). These are significant changes in the probability of conflict. The first difference for the *Political Participation Index* is negatively correlated with conflict, but 0 is within the 90% credibility interval.

The control variable estimates provide interesting insights as well. As expected, increasing the value of *ln(GDP PC)* produces a significant decrease in the probability of conflict in all models, between 10.9% and 13.8%. It is not a surprise that civil conflict is less likely in wealthy countries. We do find that increases in *ln(Population)*, tend to increase the probability of conflict between 6.3% and 8.2% across models 2.1 through 2.5. There is little evidence based on our models that either *Ethnic Frac.* or *ln(Mountain Terrain)* has an independent impact on the probability of conflict. The impact of democracy, as measured by *Polyarchy*, has conflicting results. The variable is statistically significant

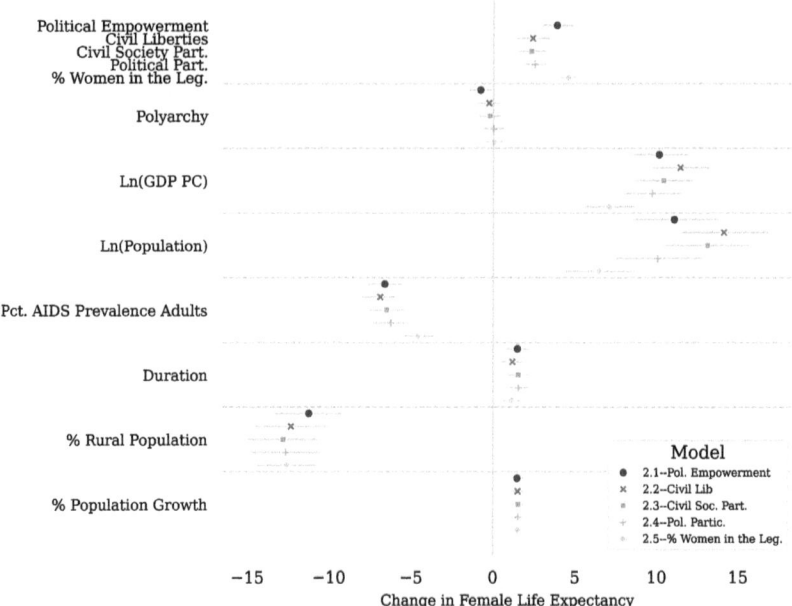

Figure 4 Female life expectancy first differences, models 2.1–2.5
Note: Posterior Medians and 90% Cr. Int.

for models 2.3, 2.4, and, 2.5 employing the *Civil Society Participation Index*, *Political Participation Index*, and *% Women in the Legislature* variables. The *N Neighbor Conflicts* is statistically insignificant in all models. There is strong evidence that having a previous conflict increases the probability of conflict. Our estimates find that a previous conflict increases the probability of conflict in a given year by over 80% in all models.

Next, we present the results of the second stages of our models, which test hypothesis 2.1. Figure 4 presents the first differences, calculated as discussed previously, of our models' second stages using the *Female Life Expectancy* dependent variable. The results are clear. In all models, increases in political equality are correlated with increases in female life expectancy in countries undergoing civil conflict. Increasing each index from one standard deviation below its mean to one over increases female life expectancy by 3.8 (*Political Empowerment Index*), 2.4 (*Civil Liberties Index*), 2.3 (*Civil Society Participation Index*), 2.5 (*Political Participation Index*), and 4.5 years (*% Women in the Legislature*) respectively. Thus, women's life expectancy in conflict countries was greater in those countries with greater gendered political equality than in those with weaker levels of gendered political equality. In addition, these findings are robust to selection effects.

The control variables provide interesting results as well. We find limited evidence that variation in levels of democracy impacts women's life expectancy in conflict countries. In fact, *Polyarchy* is negatively correlated and statistically significant in model 2.1. It is not significant in the remaining models. In all models, *ln(GDP PC)* is strongly correlated with female life expectancy, showing an increase of between 7 and 11.4 years across all five models. Women's life expectancy is correlated with increases in *ln(Population)*, adding an extra 6.5 to 14 years. Not surprisingly, our estimated increase in the percentage of AIDS prevalence among adults (*% AIDS Prevalence Adults*) significantly decreases life expectancy between 4.5 and 6.8 years in our models. In conflict countries, women benefit from stability. Our models show that increases in regime duration, *Duration*, increase women's life expectancy between 1.1 and 1.5 years. In addition, the results reveal that female life expectancy in countries with conflict is negatively correlated with *% Rural*. Our estimated increase in the percent of the rural population significantly decreases female life expectancy between 11.3 and 12.8 years in our models. Our estimate of the effect of the *% Population Growth* is consistent across all models, adding approximately 1.5 years to female life expectancy.

Conclusion

Our results in this section show that women's political equality not only reduces the likelihood of civil conflict but also helps mitigate the cost of conflict as measured by women's life expectancy. These findings are consistent with our expectations based on the existing research on gender and civil conflict. Inequality not only breeds civil conflict but also undermines women's health. These findings provide further support for increasing women's political equality in order to lessen the possibility of conflict, but also its costs.

The significance of these findings is furthered by the fact that the impact of gender equality on the costs of women's health exists even when we control for sample selection. Gender scholars have long known that gendered inequality increases conflict. Recently, scholars have considered the gendered consequences, but these studies have ignored the connection between the two processes. Sample selection affects the direction, magnitude, and statistical significance of the relationship between gender inequality and women's health.

Appendix

Table 4 Detailed parameter estimates of first stage, model 2.1

Parameter	5%	50%	95%	$\widehat{R}$
Political Empowerment Index	−3.800	−2.685	−1.603	1.000
ln(GDP PC)	−0.775	−0.576	−0.390	1.000
ln(Population)	0.217	0.412	0.611	1.000
Ethnic Frac.	−0.936	0.171	1.278	1.000
ln(Mountainous Terrain)	−0.042	0.165	0.372	1.000
Polyarchy	−0.715	0.076	0.852	1.000
N Neighbor Conflicts	−0.079	0.016	0.112	1.000
Previous Conflict	4.224	5.543	7.316	1.000
Intercept	−2.913	−2.544	−2.201	1.001
$\sigma_{country}$	1.407	1.672	1.969	1.000
% Correct	0.923	0.928	0.932	1.000
N	3,955	–	–	–

Note: Table reports the posterior coefficient and parameter estimates.

Table 5 Detailed Parameter Estimates of Second Stage, Model 2.1

Parameter	5%	50%	95%	$\widehat{R}$
Political Empowerment Index	9.520	12.476	15.547	1.000
Polyarchy	−3.743	−1.994	−0.262	1.001
Ln(GDP PC)	3.290	3.987	4.680	1.000
Ln(Population)	3.086	3.992	4.952	1.000
% AIDS Prevalence Adults	−1.993	−1.724	−1.456	1.000
Duration	0.002	0.004	0.005	1.000
% Rural	−0.290	−0.245	−0.197	1.000
% Population Growth	0.359	0.464	0.570	1.000
Intercept	67.106	68.646	70.253	1.002
ρ	−0.486	−0.271	−0.047	1.000
$\sigma_{country}$	6.508	7.302	8.130	1.000
N	651	–	–	–

Note: Table reports the posterior coefficient and parameter estimates.

Table 6 Detailed parameter estimates of first stage, model 2.2

Parameter	5%	50%	95%	$\hat{R}$
Civil Liberties Index	−5.485	−4.400	−3.383	1.000
ln(GDP PC)	−0.845	−0.628	−0.425	1.000
ln(Population)	0.180	0.388	0.608	1.000
Ethnic Frac	−1.394	−0.120	1.185	1.001
ln(Mountainous Terrain)	−0.136	0.103	0.350	1.000
Polyarchy	−0.035	0.741	1.520	1.000
N Neighbor Conflicts	−0.148	−0.050	0.047	1.000
Previous Conflict	4.527	6.066	8.172	1.000
Intercept	−3.227	−2.788	−2.387	1.000
$\sigma_{country}$	1.589	1.889	2.232	1.000
% Correct	0.925	0.930	0.934	1.000
N	3,955	–	–	–

Note: Table reports the posterior coefficient and parameter estimates.

Table 7 Detailed parameter estimates of second stage, model 2.2

Parameter	5%	50%	95%	$\hat{R}$
Civil Liberties Index	3.610	6.118	8.717	1.001
Polyarchy	−2.362	−0.682	0.890	1.000
Ln(GDP PC)	3.831	4.521	5.212	1.001
Ln(Population)	4.160	5.095	6.058	1.000
% AIDS Prevalence Adults	−2.070	−1.792	−1.509	1.000
Duration	0.001	0.003	0.005	1.000
% Rural	−0.318	−0.269	−0.219	1.000
% Population Growth	0.368	0.476	0.581	1.000
Intercept	67.433	69.142	70.916	1.001
ρ	−0.481	−0.260	−0.017	1.000
$\sigma_{country}$	7.338	8.125	8.938	1.001
N	651	–	–	–

Note: Table reports the posterior coefficient and parameter estimates.

Table 8 Detailed parameter estimates of first stage, model 2.3

Parameter	5%	50%	95%	$\widehat{R}$
Civil Society Participation	−1.939	−1.000	−0.080	1.001
ln(GDP PC)	−0.833	−0.630	−0.440	1.000
ln(Population)	0.141	0.334	0.530	1.000
Ethnic Frac	−0.941	0.157	1.236	1.000
ln(Mountainous Terrain)	−0.009	0.189	0.397	1.000
Polyarchy	−1.340	−0.589	0.168	1.000
N Neighbor Conflicts	−0.078	0.018	0.114	1.001
Previous Conflict	4.113	5.442	7.226	1.000
Intercept	−2.880	−2.507	−2.167	1.000
$\sigma_{country}$	1.399	1.666	1.973	1.001
% Correct	0.923	0.927	0.931	1.000
N	3,955	–	–	–

Note: Table reports the posterior coefficient and parameter estimates.

Table 9 Detailed parameter estimates of second stage, model 2.3

Parameter	5%	50%	95%	$\widehat{R}$
Civil Society Participation	4.058	6.212	8.433	1.000
Polyarchy	−2.203	−0.534	1.143	1.000
Ln(GDP PC)	3.425	4.112	4.814	1.001
Ln(Population)	3.748	4.724	5.650	0.999
% AIDS Prevalence Adults	−1.968	−1.689	−1.413	1.000
Duration	0.002	0.004	0.005	1.000
% Rural	−0.325	−0.279	−0.233	1.001
% Population Growth	0.380	0.485	0.590	1.001
Intercept	67.120	68.778	70.461	1.001
ρ	−0.475	−0.245	−0.013	1.000
$\sigma_{country}$	6.991	7.780	8.592	1.001
N	651	–	–	–

Note: Table reports the posterior coefficient and parameter estimates.

Table 10 Detailed parameter estimates of first stage, model 2.4

Parameter	5%	50%	95%	$\widehat{R}$
Political Participation	−1.028	−0.422	0.194	1.001
ln(GDP PC)	−0.846	−0.637	−0.443	1.000
ln(Population)	0.143	0.346	0.547	1.000
Ethnic Frac	−0.932	0.176	1.275	1.000
ln(Mountainous Terrain)	−0.024	0.187	0.394	1.000
Polyarchy	−1.581	−0.894	−0.218	1.000
N Neighbor Conflicts	−0.077	0.021	0.118	1.000
Previous Conflict	4.157	5.405	7.052	1.000
Intercept	−2.875	−2.516	−2.177	1.000
$\sigma_{country}$	1.424	1.689	2.000	1.000
% Correct	0.923	0.928	0.932	1.000
N	3,995	−	−	−

Note: Table reports the posterior coefficient and parameter estimates.

Table 11 Detailed parameter estimates of second stage, model 2.4

Parameter	5%	50%	95%	$\widehat{R}$
Political Participation	4.745	6.400	8.077	1.000
Polyarchy	−1.461	0.068	1.629	1.001
Ln(GDP PC)	3.131	3.833	4.549	1.000
Ln(Population)	2.715	3.629	4.586	1.000
% AIDS Prevalence Adults	−1.902	−1.624	−1.347	1.000
Duration	0.002	0.004	0.006	1.000
% Rural	−0.321	−0.275	−0.230	1.000
% Population Growth	0.373	0.479	0.582	1.001
Intercept	66.803	68.337	69.874	1.001
ρ	−0.484	−0.258	−0.034	1.001
$\sigma_{country}$	6.340	7.121	7.925	1.000
N	651	−	−	−

Note: Table reports the posterior coefficient and parameter estimates.

Table 12 Detailed parameter estimates of first stage, model 2.5

Parameter	5%	50%	95%	$\widehat{R}$
% Women in the Leg.	−0.026	−0.016	−0.006	1.000
ln(GDP PC)	−0.774	−0.579	−0.394	1.000
ln(Population)	0.251	0.443	0.647	1.001
Ethnic Frac.	−0.835	0.261	1.374	1.000
ln(Mountainous Terrain)	−0.022	0.177	0.386	1.001
Polyarchy	−1.597	−0.956	−0.331	1.001
N Neighbor Conflicts	−0.072	0.017	0.108	1.000
Previous Conflict	4.158	5.338	6.868	1.000
Intercept	−2.896	−2.516	−2.171	1.001
$\sigma_{country}$	1.400	1.659	1.960	1.002
% Correct	0.924	0.928	0.932	1.000
N	3,995	−	−	−

Note: Table reports the posterior coefficient and parameter estimates.

Table 13 Detailed parameter estimates of second stage, model 2.5

Parameter	5%	50%	95%	$\widehat{R}$
% Women in the Leg.	0.219	0.244	0.269	0.999
Polyarchy	−1.103	0.167	1.414	1.000
Ln(GDP PC)	2.150	2.759	3.373	1.000
Ln(Population)	1.584	2.335	3.115	1.000
% AIDS Prevalence Adults	−1.423	−1.193	−0.951	1.000
Duration	0.001	0.003	0.004	1.000
% Rural	−0.316	−0.275	−0.234	1.000
% Population Growth	0.373	0.475	0.579	1.002
Intercept	67.150	68.476	69.811	1.001
ρ	−0.818	−0.669	−0.471	1.000
$\sigma_{country}$	5.608	6.290	7.000	1.000
N	651	−	−	−

Note: Table reports the posterior coefficient and parameter estimates.

3 Maternal Health Consequences

Maternal health is an essential building block of society.[10] Countries with poor maternal healthcare systems endanger not only the health of mothers but also the health of the children they bear. When maternal health is neglected, it rebounds on the society in the form of ill-health of their offspring – males and females alike (Osmani & Sen, 2003).

Not surprisingly, improving women's maternal health remains a critically important global issue. Reducing maternal mortality was one of the UN's Millennium Development Goals and remains a Sustainable Development Goal (Alkema et al., 2016). Globally, maternal health has improved significantly over the years. Maternal mortality rates (MMR) have fallen by 38% in the twenty-first century (World Health Organization, 2017). Yet, nearly 300,000 women died during and following pregnancy in 2017 (World Health Organization, 2017). Thus, there is strong evidence that many women still directly suffer from poor maternal health.

In this section, we try to shed light on the effect of gendered political inequality on the costs of civil conflict on women's health. Again, we highlight the fact that women in conflict prone locations are likely lagging behind women in more stable societies. Thus, we are looking to explore whether greater gendered political equality can mitigate the costs of civil conflict on maternal health.

Political Inequality and Maternal Health

Public health scholars have recently begun to consider the role that women's autonomy or empowerment plays in outcomes related to maternal and infant health (e.g., Adjiwanou & LeGrand, 2014; Banda et al., 2017; Bloom, Wypij, & Gupta, 2001; Stephenson, Bartel, & Rubardt, 2012). The link between poor maternal health outcomes and gender inequality is complicated and encompasses a number of factors (Fapohunda & Orobaton, 2014; Guha-Sapir & D'Aoust, 2011; Marphatia et al., 2016; Pathak, Singh, & Subramanian, 2010). More educated women are more likely to receive antenatal care and professional delivery care than are less educated women (Bell, Curtis, & Alayon, 2003; Fapohunda & Orobaton, 2014; Pathak, Singh, & Subramanian, 2010). Not surprisingly, wealthier women are also more likely to receive better overall medical care and nutrition than poorer women are (Fapohunda & Orobaton, 2014; Pathak, Singh, & Subramanian, 2010).

Using individual level measures, research across a wide number of contexts has found a link between women's inequality and poor maternal health. Several

---

[10] Maternal health relates to the health of women during pregnancy, childbirth, and the immediate post-natal period.

studies have found that maternal morbidity is greater in those countries with higher levels of gender inequality (e.g., Alkema et al., 2016; Bhalotra et al., 2019; Guha-Sapir & D'Aoust, 2011; United Nations Human Rights Council, 2011). Most of these public health studies employ attitudinal measures regarding violence toward women and household decision-making. These measures of gender equality are based on individual attitudes as measured by survey responses. This way of thinking about inequality is related to, but distinct from, the political equality measures we utilize, which are measured at the state level.

Political inequality is important because research demonstrates that the challenges associated with lowering maternal mortality rates can largely be curtailed where the uptake of maternal health service increases (Akseer et al., 2019; Chandrasekhar, Tesfayi Gebreselassie, & Jayaraman, 2010; Chi et al., 2015b; Das et al., 2020; Mirzazada et al., 2020; Østby et al., 2018). Where women have a political voice, these services are likely to be more available and accessible. When women receive regular antenatal care, give birth in health care facilities, and have a medical professional present, many of the risks of maternal mortality can be diminished, if not eliminated (Hogan et al., 2010; Ronsmans, Graham, & steering group, 2006).

The unequal position of women in society is often reflected in their weak position politically. Existing research finds strong evidence that women's political inequality is linked to poor health outcomes in several ways. Societies that do not embrace women's empowerment have greater levels of maternal mortality and ill-health.

Maternal Health and Conflict

The existing research on the relationship between civil conflict and maternal health finds strong evidence that conflict has significant, negative effects on maternal health (e.g., Kotsadam & Østby, 2019; Kottegoda, Samuel, & Emmanuel, 2008; Tamura et al., 2012; Urdal & Che, 2013).[11] The explanations for these correlations are, not surprisingly, complex and varied.

Scholars have found that conflict often increases fertility (Nepal, Halla, & Stillman, 2023; Torres & Urdinola, 2019; Urdal & Che, 2013). More pregnancies during a time of declining resources places an even greater strain on health services and women's health, which can lead to an increased probability of maternal death. Increased fertility is linked to the decreasing use

---

[11] The majority of these studies rely on micro-level survey data of individuals in single country case studies (e.g., Akseer et al., 2019; Chandrasekhar, Tesfayi Gebreselassie, & Jayaraman, 2010; Chi et al., 2015a; Das et al., 2020; Kotsadam & Østby, 2019; Mirzazada et al., 2020; Namasivayan et al., 2012; Nepal, Halla, & Stillman, 2023; Østby, Leiby, & Nordås, 2019; Torres & Urdinola, 2019). We take a cross-national approach in order to examine the generalizability of these findings.

of contraception, which has been found to occur during periods of civil conflict (Akseer et al., 2019; Svallfors & Billingsley, 2019).

Sexual violence during conflict may also impact maternal mortality rates. Civilian victimization strategies that target women are designed to demonstrate domination over an enemy and to compromise the purity of the female population (Sjoberg, 2013). In Bosnia, women were forcibly impregnated in so-called "rape camps" where they were raped repeatedly until they were pregnant, and then held until the termination of the pregnancy was no longer possible to ensure that their offspring would enhance the Serbian population numbers (Carpenter, 2010). In Sierra Leone, women in more than 90% of households surveyed about sexual assault in war reported that they had experienced rape, torture, or had been forced into sexual slavery (Hynes, 2004; Rehn & Sirleaf, 2002). In conflicts like Bosnia and Sierra Leone where sexual violence was used systematically as a tactic of war, maternal mortality rates will be affected. The effects may be smaller in conflicts where sexual violence was more limited, but no less important to our understanding of the ways that conflict can increase maternal mortality.

Even when the international community intervenes to lessen humanitarian impacts of war, women's needs frequently go unmet. Traditional aid agencies tend to focus on immediate needs like food, water, and shelter. Basic health care may be included, but reproductive health is seldom a top priority (McGinn, 2000). International organizations that do focus on health and women's health, like the Red Cross, and private groups, like the Gates Foundation, are often unable to operate in countries when violence is intense. On a more positive note, Gizelis and Cao (2020) find that when peacekeepers are present, maternal mortality is less than in other conflict countries.

During internal wars, states divert resources from productive sectors to violence, which causes society to lose twice over (Collier et al., 2003). One of the primary reasons that health care is diminished by armed conflict is the redistribution of public funding – away from healthcare programs and toward military spending. The effects of this diversion of funds are often felt even before the fighting begins (O'hare & Southall, 2007). Research does find that high levels of maternal mortality are often due to the breakdown of health systems (Chi et al., 2015a; Kotsadam & Østby, 2019; Tamura et al., 2012). Such breakdowns are common during civil conflict since they disrupt the availability and appeal of such services (Chi et al., 2015b; Kotsadam & Østby, 2019; O'hare & Southall, 2007; Price & Bohara, 2013, Urdal & Che, 2013). Health facilities may be destroyed, or it might become unsafe to seek out services.

Disruption of state resources for education caused by civil conflict can also undermine women's health. Female illiteracy has been shown to affect a range of women's health outcomes, including maternal mortality (Buor & Bream, 2004). The deterioration of female education can lead to less thoughtful family planning and increased early marriage (Shemyakina, 2013). Thus, when civil conflict undermines women's educational opportunities, MMR will likely increase as a result.

Beyond acknowledging that conflict is gendered in and of itself, we argue that the effect of conflict on MMR will be worse in those states where gender inequality is greatest. If women have, for example, limited access to prenatal care or professional delivery services in those countries where women are treated unequally, then conflict will only make that situation worse. Countries that have historically underfunded women's health resources because of their commitment to gender inequality and then experience a civil conflict are unlikely to boost resources for women's health. If anything, women's health funding may be worse proportionally as resources are shifted toward the fighting. As mentioned earlier, conflict also tends to increase fertility, which not only stretches the meager resources for maternal care but also places greater strain on women's health by decreasing time between pregnancies. In those societies where gender inequality is great, we expect this situation to worsen women's health at a greater rate. Consequently, we hypothesize that:

Hypothesis 3.1: *In conflict countries, as women's political empowerment increases, the maternal mortality rate will decrease.*

Again, because conflict is more likely to occur in states with greater political inequality, women in those states are more likely to experience larger negative impacts on maternal health.

Measuring the Impact of Conflict on Maternal Health

Here we want to explore whether variation in gender inequality in states in conflict leads to variation in maternal mortality rates, as hypothesized in hypothesis 3.1 We utilize our dataset that covers 145 countries between 1990 and 2019 and use country/year as our unit of analysis. We again use a two-stage Bayesian Heckman-selection model to estimate all equations.[12] Random intercepts at the country level are included in all models to control for differences in variance estimates by country. To ease convergence of the model, we mean center all continuous variables. For the second-stage variables which

---

[12] For each model, we estimate 4 chains with 10,000 iterations each and a burn-in of 5,000 iterations. Model diagnostics indicate that all parameter estimates converged. All models were estimated in PyStan 3.7 (Riddell, Hartikainen, & Carter, 2021); the analyses were conducted using ArviZ 0.15.1 (Kumar et al., 2019).

we included in the first stage, we adjust their coefficients (Sweeney, 2003). Diagnostics indicate that all models converged. All ρ parameters were statistically significant, varying between 0.976 and 0.913, supporting our decision to employ selection models.[13]

Again, the first stage of our model uses the *Conflict* dependent variable (Davies, Pettersson, & Öberg, 2022; Gleditsch et al., 2002). We use the natural log of the maternal mortality rate, *ln(MMR)*, as our dependent variable in the second stage of all our models in this section (World Health Organization, 2023).[14]

To measure political inequality, we include the same independent variables used in Section 2, taken from Coppedge et al. (2023b) and Pemstein et al. (2023): the women's *Political Empowerment Index* (model 3.1), the women's *Civil Liberties Index* (model 3.2), the women's *Civil Society Participation Index* (model 3.3), the women's *Political Participation Index* (model 3.4), and the *% Women in the Legislature* (model 3.5). We would expect that these variables would be negatively correlated with the likelihood of conflict and the maternal mortality rate.

In the first stages, we include the same set of control variables we used in our models in Section 2 – the natural log of GDP per capita, *ln(GDP PC)* (Bolt & van Zanden, 2020; Teorell et al., 2023), the natural log of population, *ln(Population)* (Teorell et al., 2023; World Bank, 2022), *Ethnic Frac.* (Fearon, 2003; Teorell et al., 2023), the natural log of each country's mountainous terrain, *ln(Mountain Terrain)*, *Polyarchy* index (Coppedge et al., 2023b; Pemstein et al., 2023), the number of neighboring states that are experiencing conflict, *N Neighbor Conflicts* (Fearon & Laitin, 2003; Gibler & Miller, 2014; Miller, 2022; Nunn & Puga, 2012; Riley, DeGloria, & Elliot, 1999), and the existence of a previous conflict, *Previous Conflict* (Davies, Pettersson, & Øberg, 2022; Gleditsch et al., 2002). Our conflict models performed well in our previous analysis; therefore, we are confident that they are appropriate for this analysis.

In our second stages, we include a similar, but smaller, set of controls that are commonly found in models of maternal mortality. We control for differences in wealth by including the *Ln(GDP PC)* (Bolt & van Zanden, 2020; Teorell et al., 2023). Previous research finds that MMR is negatively correlated with wealth (Kotsadam & Østby, 2019; Urdal & Che, 2013). Wealthier states simply have more resources to devote to maternal health. We also include a measure of the size of the rural population, *% Rural* (Teorell et al., 2023; World Bank, 2022). Access to medical care is often more limited than in urban areas

---

[13] The detailed parameter estimates can be found in the appendix.
[14] The data were accessed from www.who.int/publications/i/item/9789240068759 on May 16, 2023.

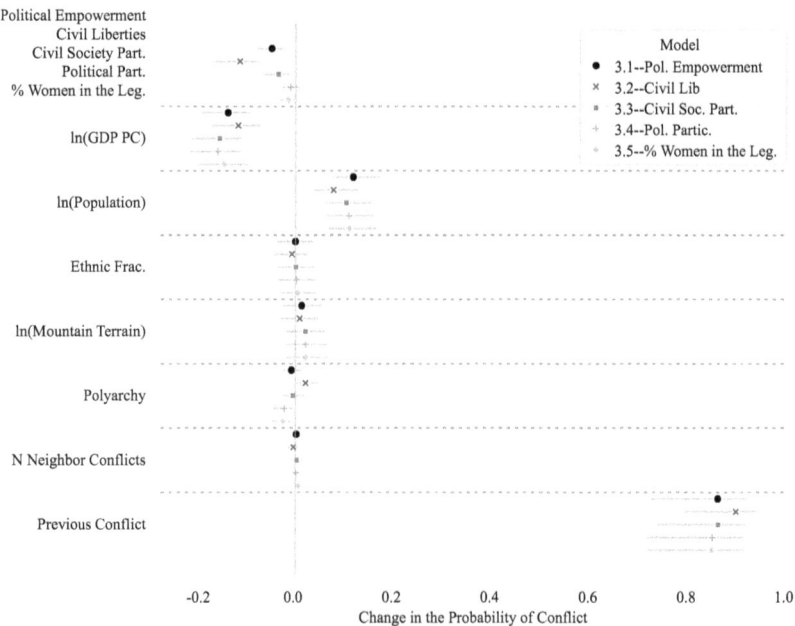

Figure 5 Conflict first differences, models 3.1–3.5
Note: Posterior medians and 90% Cr. Int.

(Kotsadam & Østby, 2019; Torres & Urdinola, 2019; Urdal & Che, 2013). Maternal mortality may vary to differences in AIDS prevalence, so we again include *% AIDS Prevalence Adults* (UN AIDS, 2023). Maternal mortality is often greater in countries where AIDS prevalence is greater (Coburn et al., 2017). Finally, we control for population size with *ln(Population)* (Teorell et al., 2023; World Bank, 2022). Increases in population have been found to lower MMR (Urdal & Che, 2013).

Figure 5 plots the posterior medians and 90% credibility intervals for the first differences estimated from the covariates included in models 3.1–3.5.[15] The first differences represent an increase in the variable from one standard deviation below to one standard deviation above its mean. The results of all models clearly indicate that increases in women's political position reduces the probability of conflict. The strength of this relationship does, however, vary across different independent variables. Increasing the *Civil Liberties Index* reduces the probability of civil conflict by 11.4%. A similar increase in the percent of women in the legislature variables reduces the probability of civil conflict by only 1.5%. The effect of the remaining variables varies between 1.0% and 4.9%.

---

[15] We used the Seaborn data visualization library to create all figures in this section (Waskom, 2021).

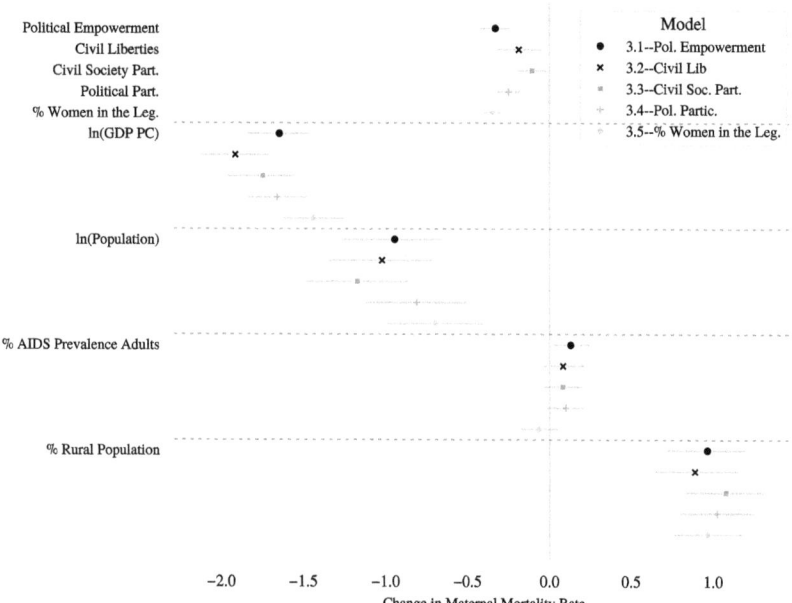

Figure 6 MMR first differences, stage-two models 3.1–3.5
Note: Posterior medians and 90% Cr. Int.

Figure 6 plots the first differences of the covariates included in the second stage of models 3.1–3.5. For continuous variables, the first differences represent the change in *ln(MMR)* of increasing the value of the variable from one standard deviation below to one above its mean. The first difference of dichotomous variables represents the change in *ln(MMR)* from increasing the value of the variable from 0 to 1.

The results clearly indicate that increasing gender equality reduces the negative consequences of civil conflict on maternal health. An increase in the (*Political Empowerment Index*) variable decreases MMR by 27.9 %. Similarly, increases in the *Civil Liberties Index*, the *Civil Society Participation*, the *Political Participation*, and the *% Women in the Legislature* decrease MMR by 16.8%, 9.9%, 21.9%, and 29.2% percent respectively. Thus, even when we control for selection, women's political equality reduces the impact of civil conflict on maternal health.

The results of the control variables provide the expected results. An increase in *ln(GDP PC)* decreases MMR by between 1.9% and 1.5%. The effect is statistically significant across all models. Changes in population also matter, based on our results presented in Figure 6. An increase in population decreased MMR between 0.8% and 0.4%. AIDS prevalence does matter, based on our results. Our estimated increases in *% AIDS Prevalence among Adults* increased MMR by between 8.7% and 13.9%. The effect, however, is statistically insignificant in model 3.5. Lastly, the *% Rural Population* significantly impacted MMR, based on our models. We estimate that increasing the percentage rural population from one standard deviation under to one over its mean increases MMR by 43–62%.

Conclusion

In this section, we explored the relationship between armed conflict, gendered political inequality, and maternal mortality. We argue that the effect of conflict on maternal morbidity will depend on the level of gender inequality within the country. Countries with high levels of gender inequality lack the interest or resources to commit to protecting the health of mothers. When these conditions exist and a country engages in civil conflict, the situation will only worsen.

Our results support our expectations – increases in women's political equality reduced the costs of conflict as measured by maternal health. We again found these results even when controlling for the fact that gendered political inequality is associated with the likelihood of civil conflict. Thus, we see a clear a link between women's political equality and the causes and consequences of civil conflict.

Appendix

Table 14 Detailed parameter estimates of first stage, model 3.1

Parameter	5%	50%	95%	$\hat{R}$
Political Empowerment Index	−3.104	−2.149	−1.225	1.000
ln(GDP PC)	−0.892	−0.691	−0.491	1.001
ln(Population)	0.404	0.611	0.832	1.000
Ethnic Frac.	−1.096	0.014	1.149	1.000
ln(Mountainous Terrain)	−0.145	0.073	0.288	1.000
Polyarchy	−0.842	−0.238	0.368	1.001
N Neighbor Conflict	−0.049	0.016	0.082	1.000
Previous Conflict	4.009	5.407	7.207	1.000
Intercept	−3.029	−2.631	−2.263	1.000
$\sigma_{country}$	1.397	1.683	2.022	1.000
% Correct	0.919	0.925	0.930	1.000
N	4,104	–	–	–

Note: Table reports the posterior coefficient and parameter estimates.

Table 15 Detailed parameter estimates of second stage, model 3.1

Parameter	5%	50%	95%	$\widehat{R}$
Political Empowerment Index	−1.397	−1.100	−0.808	1.000
ln(GDP PC)	−0.746	−0.668	−0.593	1.002
ln(Population)	−0.448	−0.331	−0.219	1.001
% AIDS Prevalence Adults	0.003	0.035	0.065	1.001
% Rural	0.016	0.021	0.026	1.000
Intercept	4.331	4.562	4.790	1.001
ρ	0.945	0.978	0.996	1.000
$\sigma_{country}$	0.947	1.108	1.299	1.001
N	709	–	–	–

Note: Table reports the posterior coefficient and parameter estimates.

Table 16 Detailed parameter estimates of first stage, model 3.2

Parameter	5%	50%	95%	$\widehat{R}$
Civil Liberties Index	−5.566	−4.426	−3.290	1.000
ln(GDP PC)	−0.921	−0.698	−0.484	1.001
ln(Population)	0.243	0.493	0.749	1.001
Ethnic Frac.	−1.495	−0.257	1.018	1.001
ln(Mountainous Terrain)	−0.183	0.062	0.304	1.002
Polyarchy	−0.002	0.773	1.559	1.000
N Neighbor Conflict	−0.122	−0.033	0.054	1.001
Previous Conflict	4.551	6.169	8.299	1.000
Intercept	−3.302	−2.856	−2.445	1.000
$\sigma_{country}$	1.600	1.923	2.300	1.000
% Correct	0.924	0.929	0.934	1.001
N	4,014	–	–	–

Note: Table reports the posterior coefficient and parameter estimates.

Table 17 Detailed parameter estimates of second stage, model 3.2

Parameter	5%	50%	95%	$\widehat{R}$
Civil Liberties Index	−0.880	−0.510	−0.142	1.002
ln(GDP PC)	−0.846	−0.766	−0.685	1.000
ln(Population)	−0.482	−0.366	−0.255	1.000
% AIDS Prevalence Adults	−0.009	0.022	0.056	1.000
% Rural	0.014	0.019	0.025	1.001
Intercept	4.416	4.689	4.961	1.002
ρ	0.035	0.607	0.979	1.004
$\sigma_{country}$	0.917	1.083	1.272	1.002
N	709	–	–	–

Note: Table reports the posterior coefficient and parameter estimates.

Table 18 Detailed parameter estimates of first stage, model 3.3

Parameter	5%	50%	95%	$\widehat{R}$
Civil Society Participation	−2.198	−1.345	−0.506	1.001
ln(GDP PC)	−0.943	−0.733	−0.534	1.000
ln(Population)	0.322	0.522	0.738	1.000
Ethnic Frac.	−1.028	0.037	1.133	1.000
ln(Mountainous Terrain)	−0.097	0.108	0.319	1.000
Polyarchy	−0.804	−0.164	0.469	1.000
N Neighbor Conflict	−0.047	0.021	0.090	1.001
Previous Conflict	4.041	5.410	7.183	1.000
Intercept	−2.975	−2.574	−2.233	1.001
$\sigma_{country}$	1.389	1.662	1.988	1.000
% Correct	0.918	0.924	0.929	1.001
N	4,104	–	–	–

Note: Table reports the posterior coefficient and parameter estimates.

Table 19 Detailed parameter estimates of second stage, model 3.3

Parameter	5%	50%	95%	$\widehat{R}$
Civil Society Participation	−0.546	−0.309	−0.075	1.000
ln(GDP PC)	−0.791	−0.708	−0.628	1.000
ln(Population)	−0.534	−0.416	−0.303	1.001
% AIDS Prevalence Adults	−0.010	0.022	0.052	1.000
% Rural	0.018	0.023	0.029	1.001
Intercept	4.304	4.550	4.794	1.001
ρ	0.789	0.948	0.993	1.001
$\sigma_{country}$	0.983	1.168	1.377	1.001
N	709	–	–	–

Note: Table reports the posterior coefficient and parameter estimates.

Table 20 Detailed parameter estimates of first stage, model 3.4

Parameter	5%	50%	95%	$\widehat{R}$
Political Participation	−0.923	−0.364	0.216	1.000
ln(GDP PC)	−0.953	−0.746	−0.548	1.000
ln(Population)	0.339	0.538	0.750	1.001
Ethnic Frac.	−1.014	0.051	1.109	1.000
ln(Mountainous Terrain)	−0.093	0.112	0.321	1.001
Polyarchy	−1.244	−0.693	−0.176	1.000
N Neighbor Conflict	−0.057	0.007	0.074	0.999
Previous Conflict	3.892	5.225	6.960	1.001
Intercept	−2.967	−2.569	−2.213	1.000
$\sigma_{country}$	1.402	1.679	1.996	1.001
% Correct	0.920	0.925	0.930	1.000
N	4,104	–	–	–

Note: Table reports the posterior coefficient and parameter estimates.

Table 21 Detailed parameter estimates of second stage, model 3.4

Parameter	5%	50%	95%	$\widehat{R}$
Political Participation	−0.811	−0.638	−0.465	1.000
ln(GDP PC)	−0.746	−0.673	−0.601	1.000
ln(Population)	−0.396	−0.283	−0.171	1.001
% AIDS Prevalence Adults	−0.004	0.027	0.056	1.000
% Rural	0.017	0.022	0.027	1.000
Intercept	4.372	4.602	4.821	1.002
ρ	0.948	0.978	0.995	1.000
$\sigma_{country}$	0.939	1.091	1.270	1.001
N	709	−	−	−

Note: Table reports the posterior coefficient and parameter estimates.

Table 22 Detailed parameter estimates of first stage, model 3.5

Parameter	5%	50%	95%	$\widehat{R}$
% Women in the Leg.	−0.019	−0.010	−0.001	1.000
ln(GDP PC)	−0.888	−0.679	−0.485	1.000
ln(Population)	0.346	0.543	0.749	1.000
Ethnic Frac.	−0.929	0.150	1.231	1.000
ln(Mountainous Terrain)	−0.093	0.108	0.315	1.001
Polyarchy	−1.228	−0.724	−0.229	1.000
N Neighbor Conflict	−0.024	0.041	0.109	1.000
Previous Conflict	3.906	5.247	7.057	1.001
Intercept	−2.935	−2.550	−2.200	1.001
$\sigma_{country}$	1.382	1.658	1.986	1.000
% Correct	0.922	0.927	0.931	0.999
N	4,104	−	−	−

Note: Table reports the posterior coefficient and parameter estimates.

Table 23 Detailed parameter estimates of second stage, model 3.5

Parameter	5%	50%	95%	$\widehat{R}$
% Women in the Leg.	−0.021	−0.018	−0.015	1.000
ln(GDP PC)	−0.657	−0.584	−0.510	1.000
ln(Population)	−0.347	−0.240	−0.133	1.000
% AIDS Prevalence Adults	−0.046	−0.017	0.013	1.001
% Rural	0.016	0.021	0.026	1.000
Intercept	4.425	4.648	4.873	1.007
ρ	0.941	0.975	0.994	1.000
$\sigma_{country}$	0.915	1.069	1.247	1.000
N	709	–	–	–

Note: Table reports the posterior coefficient and parameter estimates.

4 Women's Experiences in Iraq at War: An In-Depth Look

For a closer look at the impact of violence on individual women and maternal health, we consider the situation in Iraq in the early twenty-first century. As discussed in the previous section, maternal mortality rises when women do not or cannot make use of women's health services. Iraq is an interesting place to explore the importance of women's political inequality because of the differences in the laws regarding women and their experiences under the Iraqi government and the Kurdish Regional Government (KRG) since 1991. The Kurdish region gained de facto autonomy after the First Gulf War in 1991, largely to protect Kurds from retaliation by the Iraqi government under the continued leadership of Saddam Hussein. After the 2003 Iraq War, the autonomous status of Iraqi Kurdistan was officially recognized and codified in the new constitution. While the women's inequality in the Kurdish region is still high compared to the global average, it is lower than the regional average and lower than in other parts of the country (United Nations Development Program, 2020). The KRG has consistently expressed a willingness to embrace international norms regarding the rule of law, and they have made both legal and institutional improvements to benefit gender equality.

Because of the differences in women's political equality between southern Iraq and the Kurdish region as well as variation in levels of violence across Iraq's eighteen governorates, we are able to test the inter-relationship between these two variables. Using data from a series of UNICEF surveys performed in Iraq from 2000–2018, we examine how exposure to violence influenced women's behavior and the services they received during pregnancy (Central Organization for Statistics & Information Technology and Kurdistan Regional

Statistics Office, 2007a; Organization for Statistics and Information Technology (COSIT) - Ministry of Planning, Government of Iraq, Kurdistan Regional Statistics Office, and UNICEF, 2011, 2019; Republic of Iraq Planning Commission, the Central Statistical Organization and United Nations Children's Fund, 2000).

In addition, Iraq is not a developing country like many conflict states. Instead, it is middle income country – albeit one where the standard of living has declined steadily since the 1980s due to a series of armed conflicts (Committee, 2011). Iraq does not look like the sub-Saharan African countries that account for the bulk of maternal mortality remaining in the world in the twenty-first century (World Bank, 2020). These facts make Iraq an interesting place to look at the impact of conflict on maternal mortality. Nearly 99% of global maternal deaths occur in less developed states (Kotsadam & Østby, 2019). Iraq does not fall into that category. Additionally, maternal mortality is comparatively low in the Middle East and North Africa (MENA) compared to other parts of the world.[16] Part of our desire to highlight Iraq is to explore whether or not the impact of armed conflict on maternal health here is similar to what has been demonstrated for sub-Saharan Africa (e.g., Kotsadam and Østby (2019); Østby et al. (2018)).

The Iraq War

On March 19, 2003, the United States went to war with Iraq for a second time in just over a decade. President George W. Bush presented the goals of the conflict as furthering the US War on Terrorism and quelling Iraq's quest for weapons of mass destruction. On the military side, planners believed that the initial "Shock and Awe" air campaign would bring a quick end to the war. Instead, fighting continued for more than eight years. US troops exited Iraq in 2011, but violence continued as the Iraqi government faced continuing challenges from the extremist Islamic State (2013–2017).

During this period, the Iraqi people experienced both international and internal conflict. Figure 7 plots battlefield deaths from 1990 to 2022 (Davies, Pettersson, & Öberg, 2023; Gleditsch et al., 2002). The largest spike in deaths occurs in 2012 with smaller spikes around the 2003 Iraq War and sectarian violence both in 2005–2007 (associated with sectarian militias) and again in 2017–18 (both associated with ISIS). The hardship and death resulting from 2003 War has been less concentrated but more prolonged (Pettersson & Öberg, 2020).

---

[16] Maternal mortality is highest in sub-Saharan Africa followed by South Asia, East Asia, and the Pacific, then Russia and former Eastern Bloc, then MENA and Latin America (Ronsmans, Graham, & steering group, 2006).

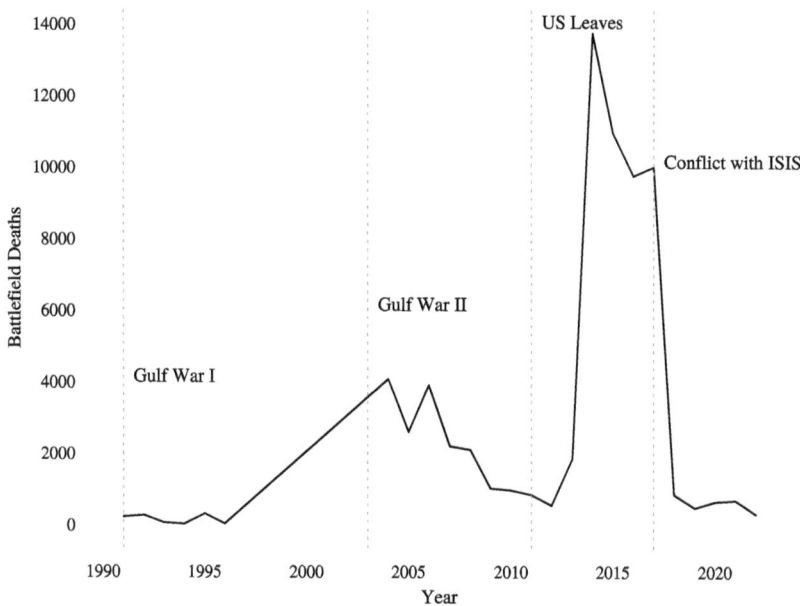

Figure 7 Iraq casualties, 1990–2022

Examining the impact of the 2003 war on Iraqi women in isolation is difficult. First the Iran–Iraq War (1980–1988) and then the 1991 Gulf War devastated the country's economy, educational system, and physical infrastructure – all of which were relatively more advanced compared to other Middle Eastern countries at the time. The decade of sanctions that followed the Gulf War limited desperately needed rebuilding efforts. The country that the US invaded in 2003 was a shadow of its former self, a fact that further hobbled the reconstruction plans for the post-Saddam Iraq. The social and political progress of the state has been slow and uneven since 2003. Unfortunately, women might be the biggest losers in the current and future political map of Iraq (Al-Ali, 2005; Al-Ali & Pratt, 2009). In societies under threat, the welfare of women is often pushed aside in favor of national security and the sense of threat serves to reinforce gender stereotypes (Tir & Bailey, 2017). Despite efforts to bring more women into the new Iraqi government, the social and political priorities of women have continually been pushed to the back burner (Enloe, 2010). Women have been excluded from key executive positions since 2003.

Women's Well-Being in Iraq over Time

The recent war in Iraq has hit women and gender relations in Iraq particularly hard (Al-Ali, 2005). Understanding the position of women in Iraqi society is a complicated proposition. The position of women in Iraqi society has fluctuated

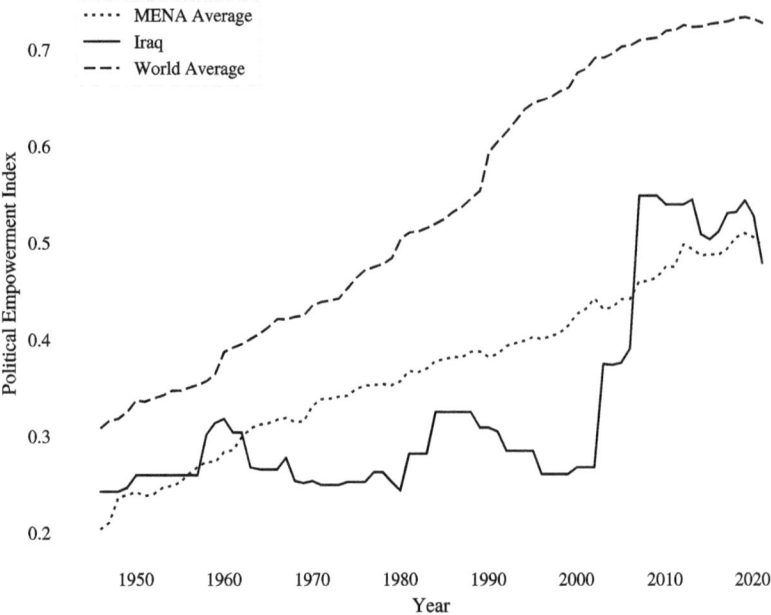

Figure 8 *Women's Political Empowerment Index* – Iraq, MENA, and the World, 1945–2022

over time. In the early years of the Ba'ath Party rule (beginning with a coup in 1968), women experienced economic, social, and political advancement that was unprecedented in the region (Joseph, 1991). The Ba'ath Party's grounding in socialism and desire to advance the economy led to the passage of several laws in the 1970s, which strengthened the position of women in Iraqi society (Joseph, 1991). This progress was enhanced by the oil boom of the 1970s. Unlike many other Gulf countries, Iraq opted to rely on domestic, rather than foreign, workers as the economy expanded, which opened the door for the introduction of many Iraqi women into the workforce (Brand, 2010).

Women's political empowerment globally and in the region has gradually but consistently improved since the end of World War II, but Iraqi women's experience has been more varied. Figure 8 plots V-Dem *Women's Political Empowerment Index* between 1945 and 2022 for Iraq as well as averages for all MENA and the world. Within Iraq itself, there is also variation between the social, political, and educational opportunities for Iraqi women in rural versus urban areas (World Bank, 2020).

Before the Gulf War, Iraq had one of the most extensive and advanced health care systems in the region as well as good water and sanitation systems. In 1991, Iraq had infrastructure that was more modern and socially advanced than nearly any other country in the Middle East (Dewachi & Berman, 2011). Much of those advances were lost to the massive bombing campaigns during the Persian Gulf War as civilian infrastructure was a prominent target category. In 1993, it was reported that Iraq was only able to produce power at about 4% of its prewar capacity (Cainkar, 1993). Without electricity, water purification was impossible, sewage could not be processed, and hospitals had only limited capabilities based on generators. Exposure to raw sewage and contaminated water contributed to the rise in communicable diseases.

Following three destructive wars and demoralizing sanctions, women in Iraq found themselves in a precarious position in the early decades of the twenty-first century. The standard of living for Iraqi families diminished, disease was rampant, and female access to education and employment were further hindered due to the rise of social and religious conservatism in the country. Gender quotas were instituted for the new national government, but women were not always given a meaningful voice in the creation of policy (Enloe, 2010).

Traditional gender roles are strong in Iraq, and they have become more dominant as the society has become progressively more socially and politically conservative since the 1991 Gulf War (Al-Ali, 2007). Women who had worked in hospitals and schools before the 1991 war often found themselves unemployed because the government lacked the resources to rebuild the facilities (Enloe, 2010). Those women who worked in facilities that survived the air strikes often found that their jobs or at least their salaries were cut much more quickly than their male counterparts, who were thought to need to keep their jobs in order to support their households.

The 1991 War was followed by a decade of crushing economic sanctions that further degraded health care in Iraq. Medical care, medicines, clean water, and healthy food were hard to come by during the 1990s. By 2002, even though the sanctions had not been lifted, life in Iraq had settled into a harsh, but predictable, rhythm. Life for women in Iraq, however, shifted once again when the United States decided that the next front in its War on Terror would be Iraq.

While the 2003 invasion of Iraq and overthrow of the regime of Saddam Hussein were achieved quickly, the reconstruction of the Iraq state was a challenging process for which the Coalition forces seemed ill-prepared. Many in the US government grossly over estimated the state of the Iraqi economy and the distribution of wealth within the society. The oil boom of the 1970s created a sizable middle class in Iraq, and a great deal of hope was placed on this middle class in the planning for the democratization of the state. Unfortunately, that middle class no longer existed. Sanctions and the hyperinflation that went along with it required most middle-class families to liquidate their assets (Mazaheri, 2010). Most professionals had fled the country in the 1990s, and by 2003, close to half of the adult population was illiterate (Allawi, 2007).

According to the World Health Organization (2017), Iraq falls in the middle of the distribution of its region (Eastern Mediterranean) in terms of percentage of births attended by a professional. In Iraq, the percentage of births attended by professionals is greater than Yemen and Afghanistan, though it does not reach the high water mark of Qatar and the UAE. The maternal mortality rate in 2019 was 79 per thousand live births.

Fertility in Iraq is high – second highest in the Arab world behind Yemen (United Nations Population Fund, 2021). Due to the weak reproductive health/family planning services and the prevailing poverty, improving maternal and women's health in Iraq continues to be a challenge.

Between 2000 and 2018 (the period covered by the available data), the people of Iraq experienced international sanctions, a war against the United States, the fall of the Ba'athist regime, internal violence by militant groups operating in the resultant political void, and the rise of ISIS and its aggressive actions to create an Islamic caliphate. The frequency and intensity of violence in the country varied over time and by location during this period, but violence was pervasive.

A Closer Look at Kurdistan

Following the end of 1991 Gulf War, the United States and the UK established a no-fly zone in northern Iraq to protect the Kurdish minority from retribution from the regime of Saddam Hussein. The protection and stability guaranteed by the Western allies allowed political parties to hold parliamentary and presidential elections and establish the Kurdish Regional Government (KRG), an autonomous government for Kurdistan in Iraq (Jude 2017).[17] Under the KRG, Kurdish women were able to organize and participate politically (Bagheri, 2022). This stood in stark contrast to the experience of women in the rest of Iraq whose political space was further limited by the instability following the Persian Gulf War and crackdowns by the regime in the aftermath.

Prior to 1991, government spending and service provision for women's health in the Kurdish governorates was limited. Providing governmental resources of any kind to the region was not a priority for the Hussein government, and when resources were provided, women's health was a low priority (Kaya, 2017). Like the rest of the country, the Kurdish region was still reeling from costs associated with and aftermath of the Iran–Iraq War (1980–1989), the Persian Gulf War (1991), and UN Sanctions (1990–2003). In the 1990s,

---

[17] Tensions still existed in the Kurdish area due to rivalry and violence between the two leading Kurdish political parties – the Patriotic Union of Kurdistan (PUK) and the Kurdistan Democratic Party (KDP). The potential for greater economic growth and deeper political investment were hindered by Kurdish groups jockeying position in the mid-late 1990s (Natali, 2010).

international financial assistance mitigated some of the impact of sanctions in the region. Aid money increased the available resources, and over time, women's activism put more women's issues on the table. While women's roles in public life across Iraq were limited by cultural norms and religious traditions, there was more political space for women under the KRG. Women were actively involved in the rebuilding of civil society under the KRG and formed a network of women's organizations across party lines to enhance the role of women in the region (Pina, 2007). They also held a small number of seats in the first parliament in 1992 (7%), but their representation has grown to nearly a third by the third parliamentary elections in 2012 (Bagheri, 2022).

The generous flow of external aid to the region (compared to aid receipts in the rest of the country) during the 1990s increased Kurdish leverage vis-a-vis the capital, which in turn enhanced the region's political autonomy (Natali, 2010). When the new Iraqi constitution was adopted in 2005, the autonomous status of the Kurdish north was codified. On the other hand, funding for the Kurdish north had lagged behind the rest of Iraq prior to the 1991 war, so much of the international funding went to humanitarian relief for Kurdish refugees fleeing from the south and to big infrastructure projects. Improvements in education, health, and economic development came along more slowly because of longer-term structural deficiencies.

Just over a decade later, international war came to Iraq again. As mentioned earlier, gender inequality in south and central Iraq has been high since the 2003 war. In the immediate aftermath, the rise in extremism and the deterioration of economic and social conditions led to increased violence against women and the restriction of women's freedom of movement in public places. In contrast, however, gender equality is relatively higher in Kurdistan (Kaya, 2017, 2018). The UN Women Gender Inequality Index (ranging from 0 (no inequality) to 1 (high inequality)) takes reproductive health, labor market participation, and empowerment into consideration. According to their ratings, inequality in the Kurdish region is lower (0.48) than in Iraq overall (0.56) (UN Women, 2018). Violence against women has not disappeared under the KRG as honor killings continue to be a cultural flashpoint, especially in rural areas, but special departments and courts have been set up in all three Kurdish governorates in order to deal with issues of violence against women (Kaya, 2017).

Differences in attitudes about women's political involvement and empowerment are also being codified into law. In 2009, the Kurdish government adopted a higher gender quota for the regional parliament (30%) than the national parliament quota (25%). Women in Iraq have the right to inherit, but only half as much as their male relatives, following Sharia, which dictates that a woman's share should be half. In 2008, the Iraqi Personal Status Law of 1959 was amended by the Kurdish Regional government to increase women's inheritance share.

The healthcare system in the KRG improved in the decade following the 2003 War, in contrast to the healthcare provision in the rest of the country (Cetorelli, 2014). In 2013, the Lancet reported a widening gap between healthcare services in Kurdistan and central and southern Iraq (Al Hilfi, Lafta, & Burnham, 2013). Limited scholarly attention has been paid to the differences between maternal health outcomes in the KRG and the rest of Iraq. Because of the differences in the legal status of women, we expect women in the KRG to have better maternal health outcomes than women in south and central Iraq.

Analyzing Inequality and Women's Health in Iraq

Based on our argument earlier, we expect that the greater political equality for women in Kurdistan should translate into better maternal health outcomes in Kurdistan compared to the rest of Iraq. At the national level, conflict certainly undermined maternal health. Using data from the World Bank's World Development indicators, we graphed the estimated maternal mortality rate (per 100,000) (Teorell et al., 2023; World Bank, 2022). As Figure 9 shows, the armed conflict in Iraq affected rates of maternal mortality during the period under study.[18]

Do we find differences between Kurdistan and the rest of Iraq? To answer this question, we use the household and individual data from four nationwide survey conducted in Iraq by UNICEF. In 2000, 2006, 2011–12, and 2018, the UNICEF Multiple Indicator Cluster Survey (MICS) was fielded throughout the country (Central Organization for Statistics & Information Technology and Kurdistan Regional Statistics Office, 2007b; Organization for Statistics and Information Technology (COSIT) - Ministry of Planning, Government of Iraq, Kurdistan Regional Statistics Office, and UNICEF, 2011, 2019; Republic of Iraq Planning Commission, the Central Statistical Organization and United Nations Children's Fund, 2000). The surveys do not include the same households in each wave, and the data are weighted to reflect the complex survey design employed. The sampling methodology for all four surveys was based on an initial health and well-being survey conducted by UNICEF in 2000. We utilize the women's weights from the survey rather than the household weights.

The outcomes that we look at for Iraq are those most highly associated with maternal mortality. In the women's questionnaire of the survey, questions are

---

[18] In this section, all figures were created using the Seaborn data visualization library (Waskom, 2021).

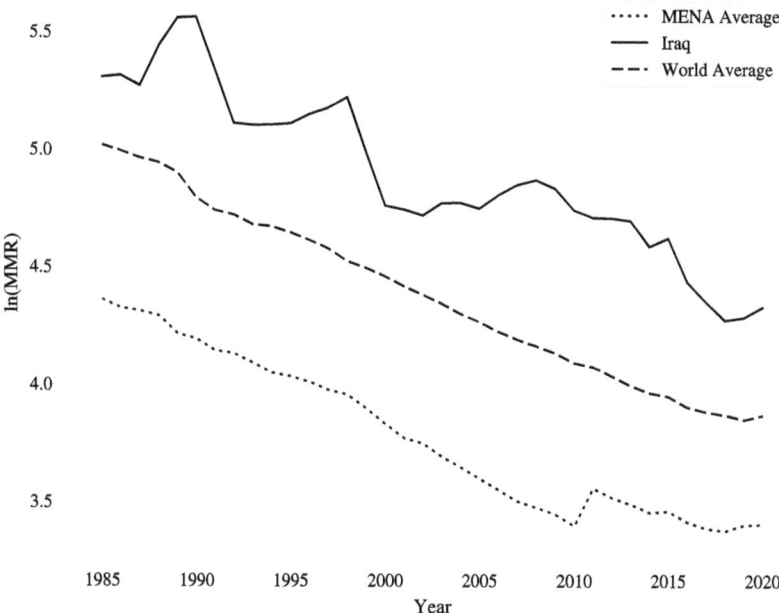

Figure 9 Natural log of the maternal mortality rate for Iraq, the MENA and world averages, 1985–2020

asked about whether or not women received antenatal care, where they gave birth (at home or in a health care facility). In addition, they are asked about who attended the birth – a medical professional like a doctor or a nurse, a licensed midwife, a traditional birth assistant or family members. Dichotomous indicators are created for whether a woman received any antenatal care, *Antenatal Care*, gave birth in a health care facility, *Hospital Delivery*, and if any medical professional was present at the birth, *Professional Delivery*. Women are much more likely to suffer complications that could result in hemorrhaging if they received no antenatal care, give birth outside of medical facility, and/or do so without a medical professional present. Based on these, indicators we believe we present a solid portrait of the risks Iraqi women faced in childbirth from 2000 to 20018.

Because all of the outcomes of interest are dichotomous, we run logit models to estimate the impact of the factors of interest.[19] To control for correlated errors within the surveys, fixed effects are included by survey years.

Our expectation is that the more equal status of women in Kurdistan should translate into better health outcomes when controlling for other factors. Thus, our main independent variable is a dummy variable, *Kurdistan*, indicating

---

[19] All models in this section were estimated using Stata 18 (StataCorp, 2023).

whether women resided in the Kurdistan governorate versus the other governorates of Iraq. Our models also include several important control variables. We measure inequality with the percent adult female literacy at the governorate level, *% Adult Female Literacy* (Central Organization for Statistics & Information Technology and Kurdistan Regional Statistics Office, 2007a; Organization for Statistics and Information Technology (COSIT) - Ministry of Planning, Government of Iraq, Kurdistan Regional Statistics Office, and UNICEF, 2011, 2019; Republic of Iraq Planning Commission, the Central Statistical Organization and United Nations Children's Fund, 2000). Next, we code each governorate in each survey year with *Deaths per capita* to control for exposure to violence (Pettersson & Öberg, 2020). Our preliminary analysis found evidence of a curvilinear relationship between *Deaths per capita* and our dependent variables so we included *Deaths per capita*^{2} in all models. We include a variable for the total number of children she has ever borne, *Children*. We expect that results may vary by the level of urbanization, so we include a dummy variable indicating whether the woman lived in an urban area, *Urban*. We also include a variable indicating whether the woman was married at the time of the survey, *Married*. Finally, we include a dummy variable indicating whether the woman had received secondary education, *Secondary Education*. All of the independent variables were drawn from the MICS surveys or their associated final reports (Central Organization for Statistics & Information Technology and Kurdistan Regional Statistics Office, 2007a; Organization for Statistics and Information Technology (COSIT) - Ministry of Planning, Government of Iraq, Kurdistan Regional Statistics Office, and UNICEF, 2011, 2019; Republic of Iraq Planning Commission, the Central Statistical Organization and United Nations Children's Fund, 2000). The detailed parameter estimates for all models can be found in the appendix.

Figure 10 plots the average marginal effects of the *Kurdistan* variable for models 4.1, 4.2, and 4.3. These models include our three dependent variables–*Professional Delivery*, *Antenatal Care*, and *Hospital Delivery*. The results are supportive of expectation that pregnant women in Kurdistan were more likely to receive better maternal health care in comparison to other areas of Iraq during the civil conflict. In all three models, we see an increased probability of women receiving a *Professional Delivery*, 1.9%, *Antenatal Care*, 2.5%, and a *Hospital Delivery*, 5.8% in comparison with other governorates in Iraq. The marginal effect of the *Kurdistan* variable in model 4.1, *Professional Delivery*, is, however, not statistically significant.

Figure 11 plots the average marginal effects for our control variables, except for the *Deaths per capita* variables. Increasing the number of children, *Children*, reduces the probability of care in all three models between

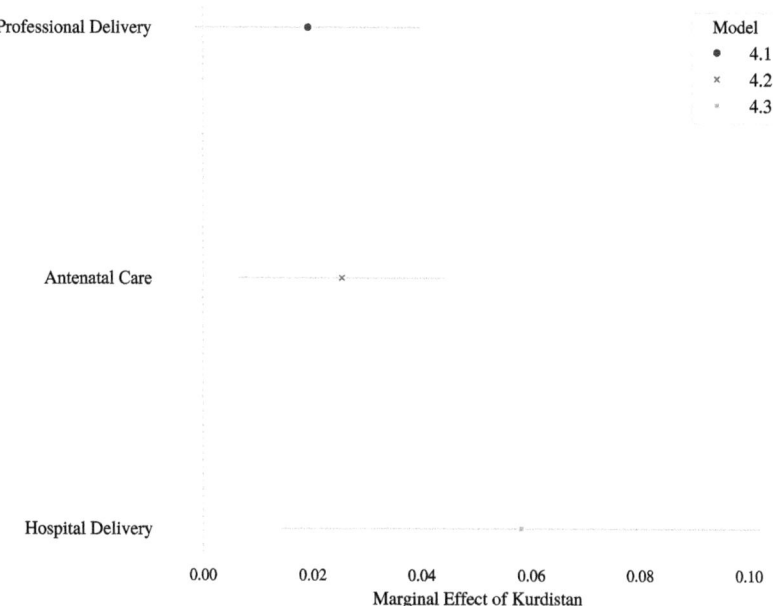

Figure 10 Avg. marginal effect of Kurdistan variable, Models 4.1–4.3
Note: Marginal effects and 95% C.I.

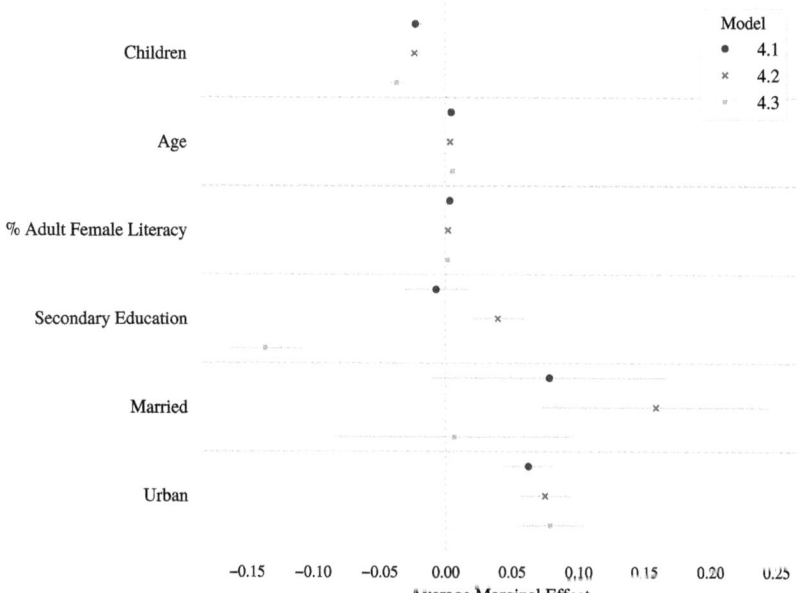

Figure 11 Avg. Average marginal effects of control variables, models 4.1–4.3
Note: Marginal effects and 95% C.I.

2.7% and 4.3%. Older women, as measured by *Age*, are more likely to receive care using our metrics in all models, though the change in probability is small between 0.3% and 0.1%. Differences in *% Adult Female Literacy* across governorates had a statistically significant, but small effect (around 0.2%). The effect of *Secondary Education*, surprisingly, had an inconsistent impact on women's maternal care. Secondary education, based on our results, had no independent effect on a pregnant woman receiving a *Professional Delivery*. Women with a *Secondary Education* were, however, more likely to receive *Antenatal Care*–1.9%. Yet, these same women were significantly less likely to have a professional delivery, 17.4%. The impact of *Marriage* was also inconsistent across our models. In all cases, the average marginal effect of marriage was positive, between 1% and 16%; however, the variable was only statistically significant for the *Antenatal Care* model. We find a strong, consistent relationship between the *Urban* variable and women's maternal health across all models. The average marginal effect is statistically significant and increases the probably of maternal health care between 4.4% and 5.6%.

Figure 12 plots the average marginal effects of the *Deaths per capita* control variable for all models. For both the probability of a *Professional Delivery* and receiving *Antenatal Care* we see small decreases as the number of *Deaths per capita* increases. Thus, as pregnant women in Iraq are exposed to greater

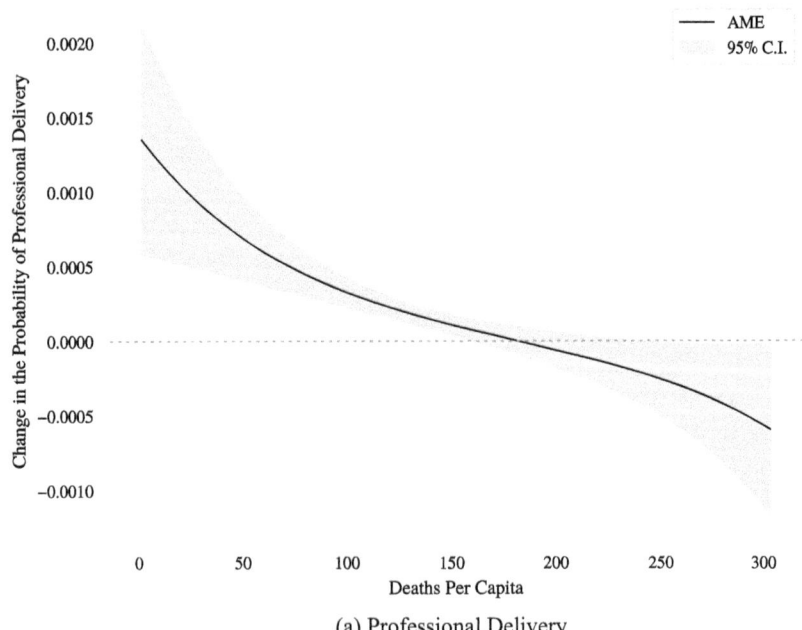

(a) Professional Delivery

Figure 12 Avg. Average marginal effects of deaths per capita, models 4.1–4.3

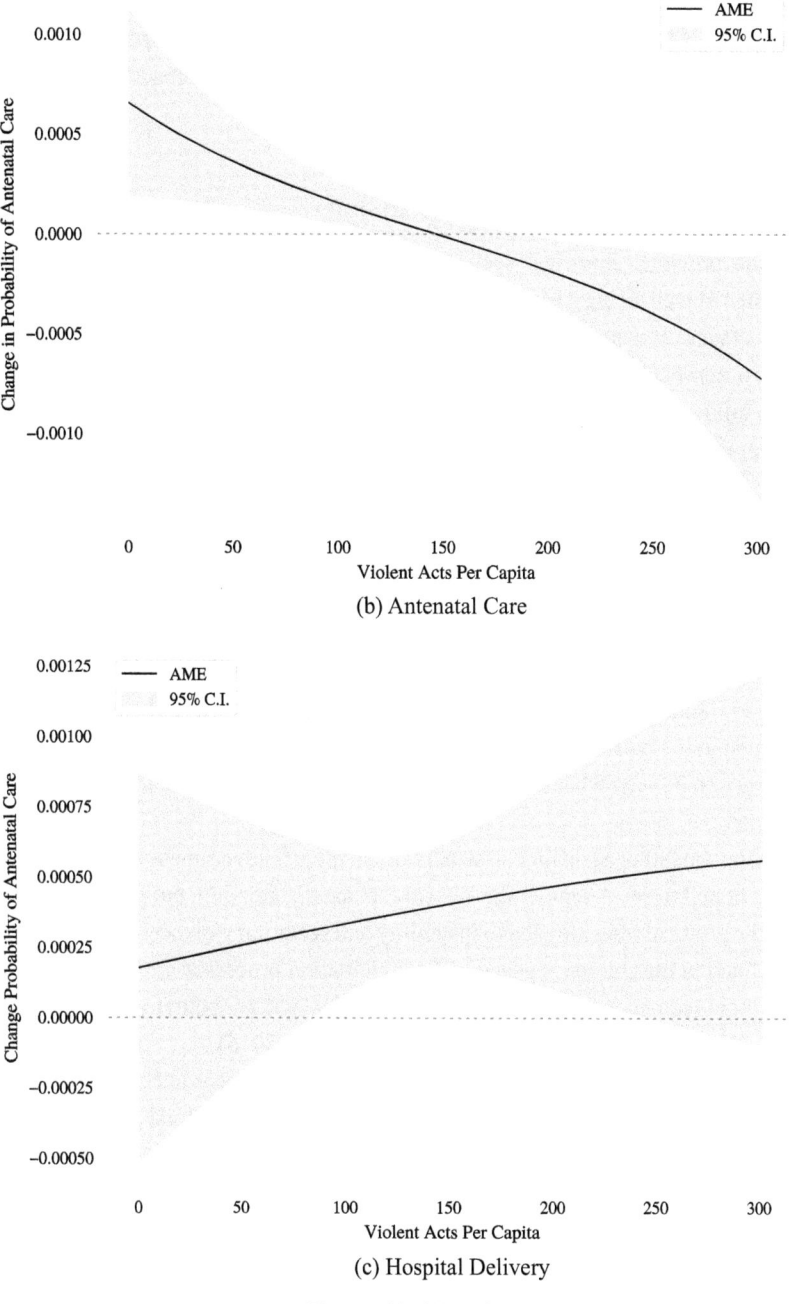

(b) Antenatal Care

(c) Hospital Delivery

Figure 12 (Cont.)

levels of conflict, they are less likely to receive maternal health care by a small amount. Exposure to conflict increases the likelihood of a *Hospital Delivery*, though the effect is quite small and not statistically significant across the range of *Deaths per capita*.

Discussion

In the previous empirical sections, we looked at the effect of conflict on women's well-being, focusing on macro-level outcomes like average life expectancy and maternal mortality rates. In this section, we took a more micro approach, looking at whether differences in political equality within Iraq influenced women's access to maternal health care. The contrast between the political environments and health outcomes experienced by women under the Kurdish Regional Government and those under the Iraqi government in Baghdad enables us to isolate the impact of women's empowerment.

Exploring the impact of armed conflict on individual Iraqi women is instructive. The devastation of the 1991 Persian Gulf War had negative consequences for all Iraqis. The violence associated with the 2003 War had much greater negative repercussions for women. Our discussion in this section also tracks the slow and steady decline of women's place in Iraqi society. The progress for women in the northern part of the country has a more positive trajectory, but it remains to be seen what the future of Iraq will look like for women all over the country.

After the fall of Saddam Hussein, many in the US government expected or at least hoped to see a democratic system replace dictatorship, but poor planning for the political transition led to instability and sectarian violence. Women were sidelined in the country's peace and reconciliation processes initiated in 2006, and there seemed to be a lack of vision or political will (or both) to bring women actively into the peace-building process (Khodary, 2016).

Our results show that women's health access was greater in Kurdistan, than in other regions of Iraq, when controlling for a host of factors, including the level of violence. This result supports our central argument that greater levels of women's political equality provide women with better health outcomes even in countries experiencing civil conflict. The unique position of women living in the KRG enabled them to have better health outcomes than women in southern and central Iraq when violence returned to the country in 2003. They were also in a stronger position when ISIS was fighting to control territory around Mosul from 2014 to 2017.

Focusing specifically on the situation in Iraq, however, we must acknowledge that this case highlights some of the weaknesses of traditional measures of political equality. For example, in 2023, there were more women in the Iraqi parliament in Baghdad than there have been since 2003, but women's rights still lag behind as the country continues to backslide on equality (Alkhudary, 2023). Despite a spate of honor killings in the early 2020s (Abdul-Hassan & Salim, 2023), the Iraqi parliament has refused to pass laws against domestic violence. While international pressure to increase political representation are an important step toward equality, these forces cannot change societal gender hierarchies and traditional values overnight.

Appendix

Table 24 Parameter estimates, models 4.1–4.3

Parameter	Model 4.1	Model 4.2	Model 4.3
Kurdistan	0.219*	0.274**	0.255**
	(0.125)	(0.111)	(0.101)
Deaths per capita	0.011***	0.006***	0.001
	(0.003)	(0.002)	(0.001)
Deaths per capita^2	−0.001***	−0.001***	0.001
	(0.001)	(0.001)	(0.001)
Children	−0.218***	−0.180***	−0.179***
	(0.023)	(0.018)	(0.016)
Age	0.043***	0.029***	0.026***
	(0.008)	(0.007)	(0.006)
% Adult Female Literacy	0.034***	0.017***	0.009**
	(0.007)	(0.005)	(0.004)
Urban	−0.067	0.318***	−0.638***
	(0.119)	(0.083)	(0.067)
Married	0.627**	0.957***	0.032
	(0.306)	(0.218)	(0.221)
Secondary	0.715***	0.666***	0.396***
	(0.126)	(0.101)	(0.066)
Constant	−1.618***	−0.854**	0.186
	(0.525)	(0.395)	(0.372)
Observations	15540	16593	16504

Robust standard errors in parentheses.
* p ≤ 0.10 ** p ≤ 0.05, * * * p ≤ 0.01

5 Concluding Thoughts

The gendered causes and consequences of conflict are inherently linked. In order to fully understand the consequences of armed conflict for women, we must recognize this connection. In this volume, we have explored the relationships between civil conflict, gender inequality, and women's health. Using thirty years of cross-national data, we show a strong empirical connection between the two processes. Our findings bolster the strong consensus that gender inequality leads to an increased likelihood of armed conflict (Caprioli & Boyer, 2001; Dahlum & Wig, 2020), and adds to the growing body of research illustrating the connection between inequality and conflict consequences (Buvinic et al., 2013; Urdal & Che, 2013). Our research adds methodological sophistication to consideration of the interrelationship between the two and helps to add theoretical richness to our explanations for both relationships.

Our results demonstrate that the gendered causes and gendered consequences of armed conflict are clearly related. On the positive side, as gender equality goes up, conflict is less likely, and the well-being effects of conflict for women are less costly when controlling for selection. Unfortunately, the opposite is also true, and women in societies with high gender inequality are punished twice.

While our analysis has clear methodological implications, we believe it also has important policy implications, most notably regarding post-conflict states. Designing post–civil war interventions and peace-building operations that aim to improve women's political equality is essential. Recognizing that gender equality may be degraded during war (Schroeder, 2017), international efforts to empower women should aim to do more than return gender relations to previous levels. Instead, these efforts will be most beneficial when they increase gendered political equality.

Improving the status of women can decrease the likelihood of recurrence. Thinking about the political equality this way gives even greater significance to the United Nations' Women, Peace and Security (WPS) agenda established by Resolution 1325. This international initiative for the inclusion of women in peace processes has emphasized the importance of representation as an international norm. While international norms are difficult to enforce, the informal pressure and energy created by the WPS agenda have created new opportunities for women (Paxton, Hughes, & Barnes, 2020). Scholars are also beginning to empirically demonstrate the negative consequences of limiting women's roles in peace negotiations and post-conflict state and institution building (Krause, Krause, & Bränfors, 2018).

On the ground, international peacekeeping missions can directly create opportunities for women's political empowerment as they provide assistance in developing new constitutions and reforming existing institutions. Bush (2011) highlights the influence of post-conflict peace-building on the introduction of gender quotas in legislatures. Efforts to include more female peacekeepers also have a demonstration effect to improve gender equality as well as increasing local women's access to the security sector (Karim & Beardsley, 2013, 2017).

More generally, armed conflict serves as a social disruption. Thus, war creates unique opportunities for improvements in women's empowerment (Bakken & Buhaug, 2021; Hughes & Tripp, 2015). Armed conflict often shakes up the societal order and reorders political systems, especially in the short and medium term (Webster, Chen, & Beardsley, 2019). Historically, war has created new opportunities for women in the workforce. Conflict often brings women out of the home and into more public spaces, amplifying their voices and encouraging their participation in political processes outside the home. Additionally, after one side has been vanquished on the battlefield, there is room for new voices to come to power.

Women who participate in social movements during conflict may gain leadership experience (Baldez, 2003). Anti-war protests or human rights movements may give women a new political voice as occurred with the Mothers of the Plaza de Mayo in Argentina and the Association of Families of the Detained-Disappeared in Chile (Waylen, 1994). Learning to navigate political spaces during times of societal upheaval empowers women in new ways. The rise in the number of female combatants has been linked by some to women's desire for greater political voice and agency (Shrestha & Thapa, 2007). Women who experienced sexual violence during conflict are also more likely to make demands for political representation in order to reform the system (Agerberg & Kreft, 2020).

Previous scholarship has focused on gender inequality as a general concept. Part of the contribution in this Element is to think about how political inequality specifically affects the way that women experience conflict. Our results suggest that countries that make improvements in women's political empowerment are more likely to avoid conflict or more importantly, additional future conflict. If and when, these countries do engage in conflict, the gendered well-being consequences can be mitigated.

Women's political empowerment has also been linked to a more effective, durable peace (Best, Shair Rosenfield, & Wood, 2019; Hudson & Den Boer, 2002; Hudson et al., 2012; Shair-Rosenfield & Wood 2017). This is a hopeful finding as many post-conflict peace-building efforts include increasing women's political participation. This was the case in Rwanda following the deadly civil war there. In 2022, women held 61% of seats in the Rwandan national legislature. In Liberia, Ellen Johnson Sirleaf campaigned and won that country's presidency on the promise that a woman could provide a different and better form of leadership after the long and painful war her country experienced in the 1990s and early 2000s.

Even small changes can have meaningful well-being effects for women. Legislative candidate quotas reduce maternal mortality and increase women's labor force participation (Dimitrova-Grajzl & Obasanjo, 2019). Unfortunately, while these reforms are meaningful indicators of women's political empowerment in some countries (Tripp, 2015), in others (including Iraq), women are not always given a meaningful voice in the creation of policy despite being allotted seats in Parliament (Enloe, 2010).

Not all post-conflict societies experience lasting empowerment for women. In societies like Afghanistan where legislative quotas were instituted to enhance women's political violence, women in politics were often the targets of violence (Bigio & Vogelstein, 2020). In the longer term, the return of the Taliban has put an end to this brief era of empowerment.

As evidenced by the Millennium and Sustainable Development Goals, the international community has placed an emphasis on women's health and in decreasing maternal mortality, especially in less developed countries – which have less capacity to improve the needed services and access to those services. Progress has been made but maternal mortality rates are still high in areas with high gender inequality and in former conflict countries. Our results suggest that one way to help combat this problem is to make women's health and antenatal care a priority in the response to civil war. These countries are unlikely to do so themselves, and thus the international community made need to help fill this gap. Healthier mothers and healthier women in general will be better partners in peace for rebuilding post-conflict societies. Gender equality is an essential element of lasting peace.

References

Abdul-Hassan, A., & Salim, S. (2023, December). *Iraqis protest gender violence after Youtube star killed.* https://apnews.com/article/iraq-government-crime-womens-rights-7ad0d8f321cce229e0f5d240679587bd.

Adjiwanou, V., & LeGrand, T. (2014). Gender inequality and the use of maternal healthcare services in rural sub-Saharan Africa. *Health & Place, 29*, 67–78.

Agerberg, M., & Kreft, A.-K. (2020). Gendered conflict, gendered outcomes: The politicization of sexual violence and quota adoption. *Journal of Conflict Resolution, 64*(2–3), 290–317.

Akseer, N., Rizvi, A., Bhatti, Z. et al. (2019). Association of exposure to civil conflict with maternal resilience and maternal and child health and health system performance in Afghanistan. *JAMA Network Open, 2*(11), e1914819–e1914819.

Al-Ali, N. (2005). Reconstructing gender: Iraqi women between dictatorship, war, sanctions and occupation. *Third World Quarterly, 26*(4–5), 739–758.

Al-Ali, N. S. (2007). *Iraqi women: Untold stories from 1948 to the present.* London: Zed Books.

Al-Ali, N., & Pratt, N. (2009). *What kind of liberation?: Women and the occupation of Iraq.* Berkley: University of California Press.

Al Hilfi, T. K., Lafta, R., & Burnham, G. (2013). Health services in Iraq. *The Lancet, 381*(9870), 939–948.

Alkema, L., Chou, D., Hogan, D. et al. (2016). Global, regional, and national levels and trends in maternal mortality between 1990 and 2015, with scenario-based projections to 2030: A systematic analysis by the un maternal mortality estimation inter-agency group. *The Lancet, 387*(10017), 462–474.

Alkhudary, T. (2023, December). *As Iraq backslides on gender equality, where are its women MPs?* www.aljazeera.com/opinions/2023/9/9/as-iraq-backslides-on-gender-equality-where-are-its-women-mps.

Allawi, A. (2007). *The occupation of Iraq: Winning the war, losing the peace.* New Haven, CT: Yale University Press.

Allen, S., & Lektzian, D. (2013, January). Economic sanctions: A blunt instrument? *Journal of Peace Research, 50*(1), 121–135.

Amowitz, L. L., Heisler, M., & Iacopino, V. (2003). A population-based assessment of women's mental health and attitudes toward women's human rights in Afghanistan. *Journal of Women's Health, 12*(6), 577–587.

Ashford, M.-W. (2008). The impact of war on women. In B. Levy & V. Sidel (Eds.), *War and public health*. Oxford University Press, pp. 193–206.

Bagheri, S. (2022). Gender equality in the decision-making processes of post-war societies: Evidence from Iraqi Kurdistan. *Journal of Human Rights Practice, 14*(2), 622–647.

Bakken, I. V., & Buhaug, H. (2021). Civil war and female empowerment. *Journal of Conflict Resolution, 65*(5), 982–1009.

Baldez, L. (2003). Women's movements and democratic transition in Chile, Brazil, East Germany, and Poland. *Comparative Politics, 35*(3), 253–272.

Banda, P. C., Odimegwu, C. O., Ntoimo, L. F., & Muchiri, E. (2017). Women at risk: Gender inequality and maternal health. *Women & Health, 57*(4), 405–429.

Baum, M., & Lake, D. (2003). The political economy of growth: Democracy and human capital. *American Journal of Political Science, 47*(2), 333–347.

Beer, C. (2009). Democracy and gender equality. *Studies in Comparative International Development, 44*, 212–227.

Bell, J., Curtis, S., & Alayon, S. (2003). *Trends in delivery care in six countries*. DHS Analytical Studies No. 7. Calverton, MD: ORC Macro and the International Research Partnership for Safe Attendance for Everyone (SAFE). [Other].

Bendavid, E., Boerma, T., Akseer, N. et al. (2021). The effects of armed conflict on the health of women and children. *The Lancet, 397*(10273), 522–532.

Bentley, R., & Kavanagh, A. M. (2008). Gender equity and women's contraception use. *Australian Journal of Social Issues, 43*(1), 65–80.

Berdal, M. (2005). Beyond greed and grievance–and not too soon. *Review of International studies, 31*(4), 687–698.

Bergh, A., & Nilsson, T. (2010). Good for living? On the relationship between globalization and life expectancy. *World Development, 38*(9), 1191–1203. www.sciencedirect.com/science/article/pii/S0305750X10000483, https://doi.org/10.1016/j.worlddev.2010.02.020.

Best, R. H., Shair-Rosenfield, S., & Wood, R. M. (2019). Legislative gender diversity and the resolution of civil conflict. *Political Research Quarterly, 72*(1), 215–228.

Bhalotra, S., Clarke, D., Gomes, J., & Venkataramani, A. (2019). Maternal mortality and women's political participation. *MedRxiv*, 19000570.

Bhalotra, S., & Clots-Figueras, I. (2014). Health and the political agency of women. *American Economic Journal: Economic Policy, 6*(2), 164–97.

Bigio, J., & Vogelstein, R. (2020). Women under attack: The backlash against female politicians. *Foreign Affairs, 99*, 131–138.

Bjarnegård, E., & Melander, E. (2011). Disentangling gender, peace and democratization: The negative effects of militarized masculinity. *Journal of Gender Studies*, *20*(2), 139–154.

Bjarnegård, E., Melander, E., Bardall, G. et al. (2015). Gender, peace and armed conflict. *SIPRI Yearbook*, 101–108.

Blattman, C., & Miguel, E. (2010). Civil war. *Journal of Economic Literature*, *48*(1), 3–57.

Bloom, S. S., Wypij, D., & Gupta, M. D. (2001). Dimensions of women's autonomy and the influence on maternal health care utilization in a north Indian city. *Demography*, *38*(1), 67–78.

Bohara, A. K., Mitchell, N. J., & Nepal, M. (2006). Opportunity, democracy, and the exchange of political violence a subnational analysis of conflict in Nepal. *Journal of Conflict Resolution*, *50*(1), 108–128.

Böhmelt, T., & Spilker, G. (2020). *Selection bias in political science & international relations applications*. Thousand Oaks: SAGE.

Bolt, J., & van Zanden, L. (2020). *Maddison project database, version 2020 [Maddioson style estimates of the development of the world economy: A new 2020 update]*. www.rug.nl/ggdc/historicaldevelopment/maddison/research.

Bolzendahl, C., & Brooks, C. (2007). Women's political representation and welfare state spending in 12 capitalist democracies. *Social Forces*, *85*(4), 1509–1534.

Brand, T. (2010). *The gendered effects of violence: War, women's health and experience in Iraq* (Unpublished masters thesis). University of Arizona.

Buor, D., & Bream, K. (2004). An analysis of the determinants of maternal mortality in sub-Saharan Africa. *Journal of Women's Health*, *13*(8), 926–938.

Bush, S. S. (2011). International politics and the spread of quotas for women in legislatures. *International Organization*, *65*(1), 103–137.

Buvinic, M., Das Gupta, M., Casabonne, U., & Verwimp, P. (2013). Violent conflict and gender inequality: An overview (February 1). *World Bank Policy Research Working Paper No. 6371*, 1–35.

Buvinić, M., Das Gupta, M., & Shemyakina, O. N. (2014). Armed conflict, gender, and schooling. *The World Bank Economic Review*, *28*(2), 311–319.

Cainkar, L. (1993). The Gulf War, sanctions, and the lives of Iraqi women. *Arab Studies Quarterly*, *15*(2), 15–51.

Caprioli, M. (2000). Gendered conflict. *Journal of Peace Research*, *37*(1), 51–68.

Caprioli, M. (2003). Gender equality and state aggression: The impact of domestic gender equality on state first use of force. *International Interactions*, *29*(3), 195–214.

Caprioli, M. (2005). Primed for violence: The role of gender inequality in predicting internal conflict. *International Studies Quarterly, 49*(2), 161–178.

Caprioli, M., & Boyer, M. A. (2001). Gender, violence, and international crisis. *Journal of Conflict Resolution, 45*(4), 503–518.

Carpenter, R. C. (2006). Recognizing gender-based violence against civilian men and boys in conflict situations. *Security Dialogue, 37*(1), 83–103.

Carpenter, C. (2010). *Forgetting children born of war: Setting the human rights agenda in Bosnia and beyond.* New York, NY: Columbia University Press.

Carter, D. B., Shaver, A. C., & Wright, A. L. (2019). Places to hide: Terrain, ethnicity, and civil conflict. *The Journal of Politics, 81*(4), 1446–1465.

Central Organization for Statistics & Information Technology and Kurdistan Regional Statistics Office. (2007a). *Iraq multiple indicator cluster survey 2006, final report.* Iraq: UNICEF.

Central Organization for Statistics & Information Technology and Kurdistan Regional Statistics Office. (2007b). *Iraq multiple indicator cluster survey 2006, final report.* Iraq: UNICEF.

Cetorelli, V. (2014). The effect on fertility of the 2003–2011 war in Iraq. *Population and development review, 40*(4), 581–604.

Chandrasekhar, S., Tesfayi Gebreselassie, T., & Jayaraman, A. (2010). Maternal health care seeking behavior in a post-conflict HIPC: The case of Rwanda. *Population Research and Policy Review, 30*(1), 25–41.

Chi, P. C., Bulage, P., Urdal, H., & Sundby, J. (2015a). Perceptions of the effects of armed conflict on maternal and reproductive health services and outcomes in Burundi and Northern Uganda: A qualitative study. *BMC International Health and Human Rights, 15*(1), 1–15.

Chi, P. C., Bulage, P., Urdal, H., & Sundby, J. (2015b). A qualitative study exploring the determinants of maternal health service uptake in post-conflict Burundi and Northern Uganda. *BMC Pregnancy and Childbirth, 15*(1), 18–33.

Clayton, G., & Dorussen, H. (2021). The effectiveness of mediation and peacekeeping for ending conflict. *Journal of Peace Research, 59*(2), 150–165.

Coburn, C., Reed, H. E., Restivo, M., & Shandra, J. M. (2017). The world bank, organized hypocrisy, and women's health: A cross-national analysis of maternal mortality in sub-Saharan Africa. *Sociological Forum, 32*(1), 50–71.

Cohen, D. K. (2013). Explaining rape during civil war: Cross-national evidence (1980–2009). *American Political Science Review, 107*(03), 461–477.

Cohen, D. K., & Nordås, R. (2014). Sexual violence in armed conflict: Introducing the svac dataset, 1989–2009. *Journal of Peace Research, 51*(3), 418–428.

Collier, P., Elliott, V., Hegre, H. et al. (2003). *Breaking the conflict trap: Civil war and development policy*. Washington, DC: The World Bank.

Collier, P., & Hoeffler, A. (2002, January). Aids, policy and peace: Reducing the risks of civil conflict. *Defence and Peace Economics, 13*(6), 435–450. https://doi.org/10.1080/10242690214335.

Collier, P., & Hoeffler, A. (2004). Greed and grievance in civil war. *Oxford Economic Papers, 56*(4), 563–595.

Committee, I. P. R. S. H. (2011). *Confronting poverty in Iraq: Main findings* : Washington, DC World Bank.

Coppedge, M., Gerring, J., Knutsen, C. H. et al. (2023a). *V-dem codebook v13*. Varieties of Democracy (V-Dem) Project.

Coppedge, M., Gerring, J., Knutsen, C. H. et al. (2023b). *V-dem country-year dataset v13*. Varieties of Democracy (V-Dem) Project.

Dahlum, S., & Wig, T. (2020). Peace above the glass ceiling: The historical relationship between female political empowerment and civil conflict. *International Studies Quarterly, 64*(4), 879–893.

Darden, J. T., Henshaw, A., & Szekely, O. (2019). *Insurgent women: Female combatants in civil wars*. Washington, DC: Georgetown University Press.

Das, J. K., Padhani, Z. A., Jabeen, S. et al. (2020). Impact of conflict on maternal and child health service delivery-how and how not: A country case study of conflict affected areas of Pakistan. *Conflict and Health, 14*, 1–16.

Davies, S., Pettersson, T., & Öberg, M. (2022). Organized violence 1989–2021 and drone warfare. *Journal of Peace Research, 59*(4), 593–610.

Davies, S., Pettersson, T., & Öberg, M. (2023). Organized violence 1989–2022 and the return of conflict between states. *Journal of Peace Research, 60*(4), 691–708.

Demeritt, J. H., Nichols, A. D., & Kelly, E. G. (2014). Female participation and civil war relapse. *Civil Wars, 16*(3), 346–368.

Dewachi, O., & Berman, C. (2011). *Insecurity, displacement and public health impacts of the American invasion of Iraq*. Watson Institute, Brown University. http://watson.brown.edu/costsofwar/files/cow/imce/papers/2011/DewachiIraqiRefugees.pdf.

Dimitrova-Grajzl, V., & Obasanjo, I. (2019). Do parliamentary gender quotas decrease gender inequality? The case of african countries. *Constitutional Political Economy, 30*(2), 149–176.

Dorussen, H., Böhmelt, T., & Clayton, G. (2022, April). Sequencing united nations peacemaking: Political initiatives and peacekeeping operations. *Conflict Management and Peace Science, 39*(1), 24–48.

Elbe, S. (2002). HIV/aids and the changing landscape of war in africa. *International Security, 27*(2), 159–177.

Engels, F. (2010). *The origin of the family, private property and the state*. London: Penguin Classics.

Enloe, C. (1990). *Bananas, beaches and bases: Making feminist sense of international politics*. Berkley: University of California Press.

Enloe, C. (1993). *The morning after: Sexual politics at the end of the cold war*. Berkley: University of California Press.

Enloe, C. (2010). *Nimo's war, emma's war: Making feminist sense of the iraq war*. Berkeley: University of California Press.

Fapohunda, B., & Orobaton, N. (2014, January). Factors influencing the selection of delivery with no one present in northern Nigeria: Implications for policy and programs. *International Journal of Women's Health, 6*, 171–183.

Fearon, J. (2003). Ethnic and cultural diversity by country. *Journal of Economic Growth, 8*(2), 195–222.

Fearon, J., & Laitin, D. D. (2003). Ethnicity, insurgency, and civil war. *American Political Science Review, 97*(1), 75–90.

Forman-Rabinovici, A., & Mandel, H. (2022). The prevalence and implications of gender blindness in quantitative political science research. *Politics & Gender, 9*(2), 1–25.

Franceschet, S., & Piscopo, J. (2008). Gender quotas and women's substantive representation: Lessons from Argentina. *Politics & Gender, 4*(3), 393–425.

Fuse, K., & Crenshaw, E. M. (2006). Gender imbalance in infant mortality: A cross-national study of social structure and female infanticide. *Social Science & Medicine, 62*(2), 360–374.

Gates, S., Hegre, H., Mokleiv Nygård, H., & Strand, H. (2010). Consequences of civil conflict. *World Development Report 2011: Background Paper*.

Gates, S., Hegre, H., Nygård, H., & Strand, H. (2012). Development consequences of armed conflict. *World Development, 40*(9), 1713–1722.

Gentry, C., & Sjoberg, L. (2015). *Beyond mothers, monsters, whores: Thinking about women's violence in global politics*. London: Bloomsbury.

Ghobarah, H. A., Huth, P., & Russett, B. (2003). Civil wars kill and maim people-long after the shooting stops. *The American Political Science Review, 97*(2), 189–202.

Ghobarah, H. A., Huth, P., & Russett, B. (2004). Comparative public health: The political economy of human misery and well-being. *International Studies Quarterly, 48*(1), 73–94.

Gibler, D. M., & Miller, S. V. (2014). External territorial threat, state capacity, and civil war. *Journal of Peace Research, 51*(5), 634–646.

Gizelis, T.-I., & Cao, X. (2020). A security dividend peacekeeping and maternal health outcomes and access. *Journal of Peace Research, 58*(2), 263–278.

Gleditsch, N. P., Wallensteen, P., Eriksson, M., Sollenberg, M., & Strand, H. (2002). Armed conflict 1946–2001: A new dataset. *Journal of Peace Research, 39*(5), 615–637.

Gleick, P. (1993). Water and conflict: Fresh water resources and international security. *International security, 18*(1), 79–112.

Goldstein, J. (2001). *War and gender*. New York: Cambridge University Press.

Guha-Sapir, D., & D'Aoust, O. (2011). *Demographic and health consequences of civil conflict*. Washington, DC: World Bank.

Heckman, J. (1979). Sample selection bias as a specification error. *Econometrica, 47*(1), 153–161.

Hendrix, C. S. (2011). Head for the hills? Rough terrain, state capacity, and civil war onset. *Civil Wars, 13*(4), 345–370.

Hoddie, M., & Smith, J. M. (2009). Forms of civil war violence and their consequences for future public health. *International Studies Quarterly, 53*(1), 175–202.

Hogan, M. C., Foreman, K. J., Naghavi, M. et al. (2010). Maternal mortality for 181 countries, 1980–2008: A systematic analysis of progress towards millennium development goal 5. *The Lancet, 375*(9726), 1609–1623.

Hudson, V. M., Ballif-Spanvill, B., Caprioli, M., & Emmett, C. F. (2012). *Sex and world peace*. New York: Columbia University Press.

Hudson, V. M., Caprioli, M., Ballif-Spanvill, B., McDermott, R., & Emmett, C. F. (2009). The heart of the matter: The security of women and the security of states. *International Security, 33*(3), 7–45.

Hudson, V., & Den Boer, A. (2002). A surplus of men, a deficit of peace: Security and sex ratios in Asia's largest states. *International Security, 26*(4), 5–38.

Hughes, M., & Tripp, A. M. (2015). Civil war and trajectories of change in women's political representation in Africa, 1985–2010. *Social Forces, 93*(4), 1513–1540.

Hynes, H. P. (2004). On the battlefield of women's bodies: An overview of the harm of war to women. *Women's Studies International Forum, 27*(5–6), 431–445.

International Criminal Court. (2011). *Elements of crimes*. The Hague: International Criminal Court.

Iqbal, Z. (2006, September). Health and human security. The public health impact of violent conflict. *International Studies Quarterly, 50*(3), 631–649.

Iqbal, Z. (2010). *War and the health of nations*. Stanford, CA: Stanford University Press.

Joseph, S. (1991). Elite strategies for state-building: Women, family, religion and state in Iraq and Lebanon. In *Women, Islam and the state* (pp. 176–200). London: Palgrave Macmillan UK.

Kabir, M. (2008). Determinants of life expectancy in developing countries. *The Journal of Developing Areas, 41*(2), 185–204.

Karam, A., & Lovenduski, J. (2005). Women in parliament: Making a difference. *Women in Parliament: Beyond Numbers*, Stockhom, Sweden: International Institute for Democracy and Electoral Assistance, pp. 187–211.

Karim, S., & Beardsley, K. (2013). Female peacekeepers and gender balancing: Token gestures or informed policymaking? *International Interactions, 39*(4), 461–488.

Karim, S., & Beardsley, K. (2017). *Equal opportunity peacekeeping*. New York: Oxford University Press.

Kaya, Z. N. (2017). Gender and statehood in the Kurdistan region of iraq. *Working Paper*.

Kaya, Z. N. (2018). Gender equality in Iraq and Iraqi Kurdistan. *LSE Middle East Centre Blog, 1*.

Kennelly, B., O'Shea, E., & Garvey, E. (2003, June). Social capital, life expectancy and mortality: A cross-national examination. *Social Science & Medicine, 56*(12), 2367–2377. https://doi.org/10.1016/s0277-9536(02)00241-1.

Khodary, Y. M. (2016). Women and peace-building in iraq. *Peace Review, 28*(4), 499–507.

Kondylis, F. (2010). Conflict displacement and labor market outcomes in post-war Bosnia and Herzegovina. *Journal of Development Economics, 93*(2), 235–248.

Kotsadam, A., & Østby, G. (2019). Armed conflict and maternal mortality: A micro-level analysis of sub-Saharan Africa, 1989–2013. *Social Science & Medicine, 239*, 1–5, 112526.

Kottegoda, S., Samuel, K., & Emmanuel, S. (2008). Reproductive health concerns in six conflict-affected areas of Sri Lanka. *Reproductive Health Matters, 16*(31), 75–82.

Krause, J., Krause, W., & Bränfors, P. (2018). Women's participation in peace negotiations and the durability of peace. *International Interactions, 44*(6), 985–1016.

Kumar, R., Carroll, C., Hartikainen, A., & Martin, O. (2019). Arviz a unified library for exploratory analysis of Bayesian models in python. *Journal of Open Source Software, 4*(33), 1–5, 1143.

Lai, B., & Thyne, C. (2007). The effect of civil war on education, 1980–97. *Journal of Peace Research*, *44*(3), 277–292.

Li, Q., & Wen, M. (2005). The immediate and lingering effects of armed conflict on adult mortality: A time-series cross-national analysis. *Journal of Peace Research*, *42*(4), 471–492.

Lischer, S. K. (2007). Causes and consequences of conflict-induced displacement. *Civil Wars*, *9*(2), 142–155.

Mansbridge, J. (2005). Quota problems: Combating the dangers of essentialism. *Politics & Gender*, *1*(4), 622–638.

Marphatia, A. A., Cole, T. J., Grijalva-Eternod, C., & Wells, J. C. K. (2016). Associations of gender inequality with child malnutrition and mortality across 96 countries. *Global Health, Epidemiology and Genomics*, *1*, e6.

Mateos, J. T., Fernández-Sáez, J. et al. (2022). Gender equality and the global gender gap in life expectancy: An exploratory analysis of 152 countries. *International Journal of Health Policy and Management*, *11*(6), 740–746.

Mavisakalyan, A. (2014). Women in cabinet and public health spending: Evidence across countries. *Economics of Governance*, *15*(3), 281–304.

Mazaheri, N. (2010). Iraq and the domestic political effects of economic sanctions. *The Middle East Journal*, *64*(2), 253–268.

McGinn, T. (2000). Reproductive health of war-affected populations: What do we know? *International Family Planning Perspectives*, *26*(4), 174–180.

Mechkova, V., & Edgell, A. B. (2023). Substantive representation, women's health, and regime type. *Comparative Political Studies*, *57*(14), 2449–2481, 00104140231204222.

Melander, E. (2005). Gender equality and intrastate armed conflict. *International Studies Quarterly*, *49*(4), 695–714.

Melander, E. (2016). Gender and civil wars. In T. D. Mason and S. Mitchell (Eds.), *What do we know about civil wars*. Lanham, MD: Rowman and LIttlefield, pp. 197–214.

Miller, S. V. (2022). peacesciencer: An r package for quantitative peace science research. *Conflict Management and Peace Science*, *39*(6), 755–779.

Minoiu, C., & Shemyakina, O. (2012). Child health and conflict in Côte d'ivoire. *American Economic Review: Papers and Proceedings*, *102*, 294–299.

Mirzazada, S., Padhani, Z. A., Jabeen, S. et al. (2020). Impact of conflict on maternal and child health service delivery: A country case study of Afghanistan. *Conflict and Health*, *14*(1), 1–13,

Montalvo, J., & Reynal-Querol, M. (2007, February). Fighting against malaria: Prevent wars while waiting for the "miraculous" vaccine. *Review of Economics and Statistics*, *89*(1), 165–177.

Mooney, E. (2005). The concept of internal displacement and the case for internally displaced persons as a category of concern. *Refugee survey quarterly, 24*(3), 9–26.

Namasivayan, A., Osuorah, D. C., Syed, R., & Antai, D. (2012). The role of gender inequities in women's access to reproductive health care: A population-level study of Namibia, Kenya, Nepal, and India. *International Journal of Women's Health, 2012*(4), 351–364.

Natali, D. (2010). *The Kurdish quasi-state: Development and dependency in post-gulf war Iraq*. Syracuse, NY: Syracuse University Press.

Nepal, A. K., Halla, M., & Stillman, S. (2023). Violent conflict and the child quantity–quality tradeoff. *Journal of Demographic Economics, 89*, 1–35.

Norwegian Refugee Council. (2002). *Internally displaced persons* (2nd ed.). Oslo, Norway: Routledge.

Nunn, N., & Puga, D. (2012). Ruggedness: The blessing of bad geography in Africa. *Review of Economics and Statistics, 94*(1), 20–36.

O'hare, B. A., & Southall, D. P. (2007). First do no harm: The impact of recent armed conflict on maternal and child health in sub-Saharan Africa. *Journal of the Royal Society of Medicine, 100*(12), 564–570.

Organization for Statistics and Information Technology (COSIT) - Ministry of Planning, Government of Iraq, Kurdistan Regional Statistics Office, and UNICEF. (2011). *Iraq multiple indicator cluster survey 2011, final report*. Iraq: UNICEF.

Organization for Statistics and Information Technology (COSIT) - Ministry of Planning, Government of Iraq, Kurdistan Regional Statistics Office, and UNICEF. (2019). *Iraq multiple indicator cluster survey 2018, final report*. Iraq: UNICEF.

Osmani, S., & Sen, A. (2003). The hidden penalties of gender inequality: Fetal origins of ill-health. *Economics & Human Biology, 1*(1), 105–121.

Østby, G., Leiby, M., & Nordås, R. (2019). The legacy of wartime violence on intimate-partner abuse: Microlevel evidence from Peru, 1980–2009. *International Studies Quarterly, 63*(1), 1–14.

Østby, G., Urdal, H., Tollefsen, A. F. et al. (2018). Organized violence and institutional child delivery: Micro-level evidence from sub-Saharan Africa, 1989–2014. *Demography, 55*(4), 1295–1316.

Pathak, P. K., Singh, A., & Subramanian, S. V. (2010). Economic inequalities in maternal health care and skilled birth attendance in India, 1992–2006. *PLoS One, 5*(10), 1–17.

Paxton, P. (2000). Women's suffrage in the measurement of democracy: Problems of operationalization. *Studies in Comparative International Development, 35*, 92–111.

Paxton, P., Hughes, M. M., & Barnes, T. D. (2020). *Women, politics, and power: A global perspective.* Lanham, MD: Rowman & Littlefield.

Pemstein, D., Marquardt, K. L., Tzelgov, E. et al. (2023). The v-dem measurement model: Latent variable analysis for cross-national and cross-temporal expert-coded data. *Varieties of Democracy Institute Working Paper, 21*(8th ed). https://v-dem.net/wp.html.

Peterson, V. S. (1992). Transgressing boundaries: Theories of knowledge, gender and international relations. *Millennium, 21*(2), 183–206.

Pettersson, T., & Öberg, M. (2020). Organized violence, 1989–2019. *Journal of Peace Research, 57*(4), 597–613.

Pina, A. D. (2007). Women in iraq: Background. In A. Cardosa (Ed.), *Iraq at the Crossroads*, New York, NY: Nova Science Publishers, pp. 113–135.

Pinho-Gomes, A.-C., Peters, S. A., & Woodward, M. (2023). Gender equality related to gender differences in life expectancy across the globe gender equality and life expectancy. *PLOS Global Public Health, 3*(3), 1–15, e0001214.

Plümper, T., & Neumayer, E. (2006). The unequal burden of war: The effect of armed conflict on the gender gap in life expectancy. *International Organization, 60*(3), 723–754.

Price, J., & Bohara, A. (2013). Maternal health care amid political unrest: The effect of armed conflict on antenatal care utilization in Nepal. *Health Policy and Planning, 28*(3), 309–319.

Regan, P. M., & Paskeviciute, A. (2003). Women's access to politics and peaceful states. *Journal of Peace Research, 40*(3), 287–302.

Rehn, E., & Sirleaf, E. J. (2002). *Women, war and peace: The independent experts' assessment on the impact of armed conflict on women and women's role in peace-building.* United Nations Development Fund for Women.

Reingold, B. (2003). *Representing women: Sex, gender, and legislative behavior in Arizona and California.* Chapel Hill: University of North Carolina Press.

Republic of Iraq Planning Commission, the Central Statistical Organization and United Nations Children's Fund. (2000). *Iraq multiple indicator cluster survey 2000, final report.* Iraq: UNICEF.

Riddell, A., Hartikainen, A., & Carter, M. (2021, March). *pystan (3.0.0).* PyPI.

Riley, S. J., DeGloria, S. D., & Elliot, R. (1999). A terrain ruggedness index that quantifies topographic heterogeneity. *Intermountain Journal of Sciences, 5*(1–4), 23–27.

Ronsmans, C., Graham, W. J., & steering group, L. M. S. S. (2006). Maternal mortality: Who, when, where, and why. *The lancet, 368*(9542), 1189–1200.

Salehyan, I., & Gleditsch, K. S. (2006). Refugees and the spread of civil war. *International Organization, 60*(2), 335–366.

Sartori, A. E. (2003). An estimator for some binary-outcome selection models without exclusion restrictions. *Political Analysis, 11*(2), 111–138. https://doi.org/10.1093/pan/mpg001.

Schroeder, T. (2017). When security dominates the agenda: The influence of ongoing security threats on female representation. *Journal of Conflict Resolution 61*(3), 564–589.

Schwindt-Bayer, L., & Squire, P. (2014). Legislative power and women's representation. *Politics & Gender, 10*(4), 622–658.

Scott, J. (1986). American historical review. *Gender: A Useful Category of Historical Analysis, 91*, 1053–1075.

Shair-Rosenfield, S., & Wood, R. (2017). Governing well after war: How improving female representation prolongs post-conflict peace. *The Journal of Politics, 79*(3), 995–1009.

Shemyakina, O. (2011). The effect of armed conflict on accumulation of schooling: Results from Tajikistan. *Journal of Development Economics, 95*(2), 186–200.

Shemyakina, O. (2013). Patterns in female age at first marriage and Tajik armed conflict. *European Journal of Population/Revue européenne de Démographie, 29*(3), 303–343.

Shrestha, A., & Thapa, R. (2007). *The impact of armed conflicts on women in South Asia*. New Delhi: Manohar.

Singer, P. W. (2002). Aids and international security. *Survival, 44*(1), 145–158.

Sjoberg, L. (2010). *Gender, war, and militarism: Feminist perspectives*. ABC-Clio.

Sjoberg, L. (2012). Gender, structure, and war: What waltz couldn't see. *International Theory, 4*(1), 1–38.

Sjoberg, L. (2013). *Gendering global conflict: Toward a feminist theory of war*. New York: Columbia University Press.

Sjoberg, L., & Gentry, C. (2007). *Mothers, monsters, whores: Women's violence in global politics*. London: Zed Books.

Sjoberg, L., & Gentry, C. (2011). *Women, gender, and terrorism*. Athens: University of Georgia Press.

Spiegel, P. (2004). HIV/aids among conflict-affected and displaced populations: Dispelling myths and taking action. *Disasters, 28*(3), 322–339.

StataCorp. (2023). *Stata Statistical Software: Release 18*. College Station, TX: StataCorp LP.

Stephenson, R., Bartel, D., & Rubardt, M. (2012). Constructs of power and equity and their association with contraceptive use among men and women in rural Ethiopia and Kenya. *Global Public Health, 7*(6), 618–634.

Stewart, F., & Fitzgerald, V. (2000). *War and underdevelopment, volume 1: The economic and social consequences of conflict*. New York: Oxford University Press.

Svallfors, S., & Billingsley, S. (2019). Conflict and contraception in Colombia. *Studies in Family Planning, 50*(2), 87–112.

Sweeney, K. J. (2003). The severity of interstate disputes: Are dyadic capability preponderances really more pacific? *The Journal of Conflict Resolution, 47*(6), 728–750.

Swiss, L., Fallon, K., & Burgos, G. (2012). Does critical mass matter? women's political representation and child health in developing countries. *Social Forces, 91*(2), 531–558.

Tamura, M., Hinderaker, S., Manzi, M., Van Den Bergh, R., & Zachariah, R. (2012). Severe acute maternal morbidity and associated deaths in conflict and post-conflict settings in africa. *Public Health Action, 2*(4), 1220–125.

Teorell, J., Dahlberg, S., Holmberg, S. et al. (2023). *The quality of government standard dataset, version jan23*. Gothenburg: The Quality of Government Institute.

Theisen, O. M. (2008). Blood and soil? resource scarcity and internal armed conflict revisited. *Journal of Peace Research, 45*(6), 801–818.

Thomas, J. L., & Bond, K. D. (2015). Women's participation in violent political organizations. *American Political Science Review, 109*(3), 488–506.

Tickner, J. A. (1997). You just don't understand: Troubled engagements between feminists and IR theorists. *International Studies Quarterly, 41*(4), 611–632.

Tickner, J. A. (1992). *Gender in international relations: Feminist perspectives on achieving global security*. New York: Columbia University Press.

Tir, J., & Bailey, M. (2017). Painting too "rosie" a picture: The impact of external threat on women's economic welfare. *Conflict Management and Peace Science*, 249–262.

Toole, M. (1997). Displaced persons and war. In B. Levy & V. Sidel (Eds.), *War and public health*. New York: Oxford University Press, pp. 197–214.

Toole, M. J., & Waldman, R. J. (1993). Refugees and displaced persons: War, hunger, and public health. *Jama, 270*(5), 600–605.

Torres, A. F. C., & Urdinola, B. P. (2019). Armed conflict and fertility in Colombia, 2000–2010. *Population Research and Policy Review, 38*(2), 173–213.

Tripp, A. M. (2015). *Woman and power in postconflict africa.* New York: Cambridge University Press.

True, J. (2012). *The political economy of violence against women.* New York: Oxford University Press.

UN AIDS. (2023). *Hiv estimates from 1990 to present.* www.unaids.org/sites/default/files/media_asset/HIV_estimates_from_1990-to-present.xlsx.

UN Women. (2018). *Gender profile - iraq 2018.* https://oxfamilibrary.openrepository.com/bitstream/handle/10546/620602/rr-gender-profile-iraq-131218-en.pdf (Accessed: October 31, 2024)

UNAIDS. (2000, January 10). *AIDS Becoming Africa's Top Human Security Issue, UN Warns.* (p. 1).

UNDP. (2018). *Human development indices and indicators: 2018 statistical update.* (Tech. Rep.). New York: United Nations Development Program.

UNHCR. (n.d.). *Internally displaced people.* www.unhcr.org/us/about-unhcr/who-we-protect/internally-displaced-people (Accessed: October 10, 2024)

United Nations Development Program. (2020). *Human development report 2020: The next frontier: Human development and the anthropocene.* New York: United Nations Development Program.

United Nations Human Rights Council. (2011). *Practices in adopting a human rights-based approach to eliminate preventable maternal mortality and human rights* [Report of the Office of the United Nations High Commissioner for Human Rights].

United Nations Population Fund. (2021). *2021 UNFPA humanitarian response in Yemen* (Tech. Rep.). New York: United Nations.

United Women. (2020). Realizing women's rights and other reproductive resources. New York: United Nations and UN Women.

Urdal, H., & Che, C. P. (2013). War and gender inequalities in health: The impact of armed conflict on fertility and maternal mortality. *International Interactions, 39*(4), 489–510.

Van Lerberghe, W., Matthews, Z., Achadi, E. et al. (2014). Country experience with strengthening of health systems and deployment of midwives in countries with high maternal mortality. *The Lancet, 384*(9949), 1215–1225.

Waskom, M. L. (2021). Seaborn: Statistical data visualization. *Journal of Open Source Software, 6*(60), 1–4, 3021.

Waylen, G. (1994). Women and democratization conceptualizing gender relations in transition politics. *World Politics, 46*(3), 327–354.

Webster, K., Chen, C., & Beardsley, K. (2019). Conflict, peace, and the evolution of women's empowerment. *International Organization, 73*(2), 255–289.

Welch, S. (1985). Are women more liberal than men in the US congress? *Legislative Studies Quarterly*, *10*(1), 125–134.

Welch, S., & Hibbing, J. (1992). Financial conditions, gender, and voting in American national elections. *The Journal of Politics*, *54*(1), 197–213.

Westfall, A., & Chantiles, C. (2016). The political cure: Gender quotas and women's health. *Politics & Gender*, *12*(3), 469–490.

Wood, E. (2006). Variation in sexual violence during war. *Politics & Society*, *34*(3), 307–342.

Wood, E. (2009). Armed groups and sexual violence: When is wartime rape rare? *Politics and Society*, *37*(1), 131–161.

Wood, R. M., & Thomas, J. L. (2017). Women on the frontline. *Journal of Peace Research*, *54*(1), 31–46.

World Bank. (2020). *World development indicators*. Washington, DC: World Bank.

World Bank. (2022). *World development indicators 2022*. Washington, DC: World Bank Group.

World Bank. (2023). *Women, business and the law 2023*. Washington, DC: World Bank.

World Health Organization. (2003). *The world health report 2003*. Geneva: World Health Organization.

World Health Organization. (2017). *Trends in maternal mortality: 1990 to 2017: Estimates by WHO, UNICEF, UNFPA, World Bank Group and the United Nations population division*. Geneva: World Health Organization.

World Health Organization. (2023). *Trends in maternal mortality 2000 to 2020: Estimates by WHO, UNICEF, UNFPA, World Bank Group and UNDESA/population division* (Tech. Rep.). Geneva: World Health Organization.

Zahidi, S. (2023). *Global gender gap report*. Geneva: World Economic Forum.

Cambridge Elements

Gender and Politics

Tiffany D. Barnes
University of Texas at Austin

Tiffany D. Barnes is Professor of Political Science at the University of Texas at Austin. She is the author of *Women, Politics, and Power: A Global Perspective* (Rowman & Littlefield, 2007) and, award-winning, *Gendering Legislative Behavior* (Cambridge University Press, 2016). Her research has been funded by the National Science Foundation (NSF) and recognized with numerous awards. Barnes is the former president of the Midwest Women's Caucus and founder and director of the Empirical Study of Gender (EGEN) network.

Diana Z. O'Brien
Washington University in St. Louis

Diana Z. O'Brien is the Bela Kornitzer Distinguished Professor of Political Science at Washington University in St. Louis. She specializes in the causes and consequences of women's political representation. Her award-winning research has been supported by the NSF and published in leading political science journals. O'Brien has also served as a Fulbright Visiting Professor, an associate editor at *Politics & Gender*, the president of the Midwest Women's Caucus, and a founding member of the EGEN network.

About the Series

From campaigns and elections to policymaking and political conflict, gender pervades every facet of politics. Elements in Gender and Politics features carefully theorized, empirically rigorous scholarship on gender and politics. The Elements both offer new perspectives on foundational questions in the field and identify and address emerging research areas.

Cambridge Elements

Gender and Politics

Elements in the Series

In Love and at War: Marriage in Non-state Armed Groups
Hilary Matfess

Counter-Stereotypes and Attitudes Toward Gender and LGBTQ Equality
Jae-Hee Jung and Margit Tavits

The Politics of Bathroom Access and Exclusion in the United States
Sara Chatfield

Women, Gender, and Rebel Governance during Civil Wars
Meredith Maloof Loken

Abortion Attitudes and Polarization in the American Electorate
Erin C. Cassese, Heather L. Ondercin and Jordan Randall

Gender, Ethnicity, and Intersectionality in Cabinets: Asia and Europe in Comparative Perspective
Amy H. Liu, Roman Hlatky, Keith Padraic Chew, Eoin L. Power, Sam Selsky, Betty Compton and Meiying Xu

Gendered Jobs and Local Leaders: Women, Work, and the Pipeline to Local Political Office
Rachel Bernhard and Mirya R. Holman

What's Happened to the Gender Gap in Political Activity?: Social Structure, Politics, and Participation in the United States
Shauna L. Shames, Sara Morell, Ashley Jardina, Kay Lehman Schlozman and Nancy Burns

Family Matters: How Romantic Partners Shape Politicians' Careers
Olle Folke, Moa Frödin Gruneau and Johanna Rickne

Glass Ceilings, Glass Cliffs, and Quicksands: Gendered Party Leadership in Parliamentary Systems
Andrea S. Aldrich and Zeynep Somer-Topcu

Attitudes toward Political Authoritarianism in Economically Advanced Democracies: The Role of Gender Values and Norms
Amy C. Alexander and Gefjon Off

Conflict and Maternal Health: Linking the Gendered Causes and Gendered Consequences of War
Susan Hannah Allen and Frank C. Thames

A full series listing is available at: www.cambridge.org/EGAP

For EU product safety concerns, contact us at Calle de José Abascal, 56–1º,
28003 Madrid, Spain or eugpsr@cambridge.org.

www.ingramcontent.com/pod-product-compliance
Ingram Content Group UK Ltd.
Pitfield, Milton Keynes, MK11 3LW, UK
UKHW021959030326
468620UK00021B/810